This is for the woman who needs a little help dealing with, expressing, or simply understanding her own emotions. And for the man who seeks to better understand his woman, in order to be a better man to and for her.

@Poetic_Style

Contents

SHE SAID—

"I believed you when I knew better. Forgave, and took you back when I knew it was time to let go. Defended you when I knew you were dead wrong, only for you to find new ways to make me look like a fool again. So thank you. Thank you for the rude awakening. I needed that."

--*Too often we want to give the benefit of doubt to people who are undeserving of it. Too often we don't realize that doing this continues to put us in a position to be let down. But sometimes, that's what it takes. Sometimes, we just need to keep hitting dead ends with someone before we finally get the message.*

SHE SAID-

"I am realizing that there is a difference between love and comfort, a difference between loyalty and stu-pidity, a difference between someone who wants me around because they can't stand the thought of losing me, and someone who only wants me to stay so they can keep using me."

--*It's best you understand this. Because some people will feed you just enough bull-crap to keep you around for their own benefit and convenience. Don't devote your life to someone who only seems to be taking from you and giving nothing in return. That is not a relationship.*

SHE SAID-

"Love can be so complicated at times because of the hell it brings.

Feels like I'm fighting for someone who has already left the ring."

--*You simply can't and should not fight for someone who does not care to be won. Not only is it draining, but pointless as well. They have to show some type of willingness to be in it. Even if they aren't meeting you halfway, they have to at least show the desire to want to meet you SOMEWHERE. Otherwise you are simply wasting your time.*

SHE SAID –

"Part of me doesn't like you, but the other part loves you.

Part of me wants to fight you, while the other part wants to hug you.

You bring out the worst and the best in me.

Push me till I feel I have nothing left in me, and then convince me to stay."

--It's the power of love; the power to make us feel so many different things all at the same time. For even when we are furious at someone we love, our heart does not automatically detach from that person at that moment.

SHE SAID-

"I learned that being a good woman doesn't mean that you have to repeatedly put up with bullshit. Sometimes a good woman needs to be able to say 'enough is enough' when her heart is continuously being abused and taken for granted. So that when the day comes, she may be able to walk away without jeopardizing her character, and continue to be JUST THAT... a GOOD WOMAN."

-Don't let the kindness of your heart cause you to get used and abused by anyone. Too often our women get damaged by people who never deserved them in the first place. Some men may not be mature enough to understand this yet, but a good woman is a terrible thing to waste.

SHE SAID-

"My friends are quick to tell me that if he's not acting right, then I NEED TO GO. But if you ask me, I don't EVEN KNOW. Because, these days, it seems like you either have to put up with bullshit, or BE ALONE."

--Unfortunately, the generation we live in has made so many feel like they have to lessen their standards, because relationships have become something that aren't taken as seriously. Most people get in them just to have something convenient around, without caring for all the work that is involved in maintaining a healthy relationship.

SHE SAID-

"Not sure if I am purposely being naïve to the fact that you'll never act right, or I'm still just CAUGHT UP IN DISBELIEF--or if all the feelings I've already invested in you are what is making it HARDER FOR ME TO LEAVE..."

--A lot of times it's all three. A lot of times the feelings we already have for someone make it hard to walk away. So because of that, we choose to be naïve to the fact that someone is no good for us. Hoping that will make all our problems disappear... because we don't want to believe the one our heart chose could be wrong for us.

SHE SAID-

"I can't believe I let myself fall, hoping that you would be different, because as it turns out, you weren't. And now I'm stuck here trying to convince myself that I don't give a fuck; but I'm no good at pretending."

--Convincing your heart that it doesn't feel what it does is a task that is next to impossible. We might be able to tell our friends, and even tell ourselves how much we don't care… but no matter how many times we say it, it never seems to trick our hearts into believing it.

SHE SAID-

"As unhappy as I was, I told myself that I didn't leave because I LOVED YOU. I allowed myself to continuously get mistreated because I LOVED YOU. But eventually I realized that LOVE is meant to be a reason to be HAPPY, not an excuse to be MISERABLE."

--*Often we want something so bad that we start to make excuses as to why we have chosen to ignore the reality of what is. Knowing that accepting that certain reality would mean accepting the possibility that the thing which we desire so much, is simply not for us.*

SHE SAID -

"You tell me that you will change. And though I know it's all lies, I still managed to walk away four times… and walk back five."

--Walking away is usually not the hardest part… STAYING away is.

SHE SAID-

"Maybe there were signs and I just chose not to notice them.

But the more I sit trying to figure it out, the more I can't get over it."

--*Sometimes when things end, so many questions get left unanswered, which leads us to start looking for answers within ourselves as to why something ended. Trying to figure out what we did wrong, or why we didn't see it coming. And in most cases, all this does is make us feel even worse about the situation. Because sometimes the questions we are asking can't be answered... at least not by ourselves.*

SHE SAID -

"I kept forgiving you not because I believed you were truly sorry, but because I wanted to make use of any chance that we could still make it. But sadly, it seemed like the more I forgave you, the less you tried."

--A lot of times we want something so bad, that we keep trying over and over, even when all efforts have been to no avail. We find ourselves putting up with more than we usually would, and forgiving people more times than we probably should. But we usually never notice this until we are able to re-evaluate the situation in hindsight.

•

SHE SAID–

"I've had my heart broken many times… I just never thought it WOULD BE YOU.

And yet I'm still here with my heart wide open after all you've PUT ME THROUGH."

--They say every girl has that one guy that she keeps coming back to no matter what…

…and nobody knows why--not even her.

SHE SAID-

"Event though it hurt like hell to do so, I'm glad I left.

Because at the time, I was too caught up in trying to make it work to realize that I was choosing you over my own happiness."

--*Love has a way of making us put our own self-desires on the back burner; and sometimes, our own happiness as well. Because we become so busy pursuing happiness with someone, that we forget that that is not the only way to be happy.*

SHE SAID-

"Though you were wrong for me, I got accustomed to your bullshit and knew exactly what to expect from you. And my excuse for staying was telling myself that nobody is perfect; and this was me 'accepting you' for who you were. But the truth is, this wasn't me 'accepting' you; this was me settling for less than I knew I deserved, and not wanting to admit it."

--Always remember that settling for someone whom you know is no good for you is not better than being alone… it's worse.

SHE SAID–

"This situation has got to be the worst, because I tell you to come over after telling you how much hurt you've caused. So needless to say, moving on is something I didn't get to do yet, because how can I get over you when we keep connecting through sex."

--Sex has become one of the bigger factors in relationships of today. And it sometimes plays the major role in why some people have a hard time separating themselves from people they should. It's the comfort of having someone there for your sexual needs--someone you are already comfortable with. Unfortunately, this usually makes the moving-on process last a lot longer than it should, and in return, contributes to the amount of time wasted.

SHE SAID-

"Erasing every memory of you altogether remains something I still WISH I COULD DO.

Because even when I'm thinking of the not-so-pleasant memories, I'm still THINKING OF YOU... So eventually, I begin to miss you."

--*Being absent from someone your heart is fond of is never easy, even when it's someone you are better off without. If only our brain had a "forget" switch. It's ironic how the things that we disliked about someone often don't help us get over that person; but instead, begin to only serve as a reminder of how much we miss that person.*

SHE SAID-

"I always went the extra mile. More than giving you my all, I gave you chance after chance. And when you so often hurt me, I continued to stay through the pain. But now I'm learning that just because you're willing to do so much for someone, doesn't mean that they'll do the same"

--*We often forget that the way we feel about someone, and the things we would do for them are not always reciprocated... and in most cases, that's what makes the disappointment even more severe. Because at the end of the day, that's what it's about; being with someone who feels for you what you feel for them; willing to do for you what you would for them; and undoubtedly willing to roll up their sleeves and fight for you without a moment of thought.*

SHE SAID—

"I should have already left. I mean after all the hurt you've put me through, you'd think that would have been enough for me. But somehow I still love you more than I hate what you have done to me."

--Love is the most powerful drug; so strong that we would go through some of the worst situations and the greatest pain and still be with the person who caused it all in the name of "Love." And unfortunately, there is no ten-step program, no counseling sessions, or therapy that you can go to and learn how to quit... how to "not love" someone anymore. It's always pretty much something beyond your control. For some, getting over someone happens spontaneously. For others, it takes time...

SHE SAID-

"You were always good at knowing what to say to make me stay. And even when I knew it was a lie, I was always good at believing you."

--*A lot of times, when you love someone, you are always looking for a reason to stay. But sometimes it becomes pretty clear that staying would be the stupid thing to do, so acting as though we don't want to feel "stupid," we look for an excuse. An excuse as to why we forgave them. One that will help make our decision to stay seem less stupid on our behalf. Which is why when they say something as simple as "I'm sorry, it won't happen again," we jump at the opportunity to take them back... conveniently forgetting that it is the 37th time that they have made that claim.*

SHE SAID-

"Seems like no matter how much you break me down, I still don't want to give you up. I swear I can't stand loving you this much because there is almost no love left for myself."

--*One of the most common mistakes people make is giving so much of themselves to someone that they forget about their own needs. Love is strong; and you should go the extra mile to make it work, which often includes putting someone else's feelings and needs in front of yours; but you cannot completely forget about yourself. There has to be some kind of balance.*

SHE SAID–

"They call me silly for letting someone make a fool out of me all for love. If only they understood that my feelings do not just turn on and off… even though I sometimes wish they did."

--As the saying goes: "it's easier said than done." Often people act like it's that easy to just pick up and walk away; but the truth is, we don't have that type of control over our feelings. Especially with a feeling as overwhelming as love. Lord knows if we did, if we could just hit a switch and feel nothing for someone, there would be a lot fewer broken hearts… but something tells me if that was the case, finding true love also would not be as special and refreshing as it is now.

SHE SAID –

"When I leave, I might hurt for a while, but TIME WILL HEAL IT. And eventually, time will also lead me to FIND SOME REAL SHIT. But while time is doing that for me, it'll also teach you a few lessons that you APPARENTLY DON'T KNOW. Lessons like 'One good woman is worth more than a HUNDRED HOES."

--Unfortunately, this is a lesson that comes with maturity, and some men just don't mature as fast. Too often good women are lost by men who do not understand the concept of quality over quantity… and too often, these good women are lost forever.

SHE SAID –

"I hate that I can't control still loving you despite how different you've become. Seems like the deeper I fall for you, the more distant you become. But when I pull away, you seem to pull me back... only to later become distant again. I can't win."

--*The thing is that a lot of men are afraid of emotion, whether from themselves, or from other people. Which is why some start to pull away when they notice a relationship getting more serious than they are ready for; or when they notice themselves falling too hard for a woman. Their habits start to change, and they begin to seem "distant"... it is usually that state of confusion. Most times it's not that they want to walk away from the situation, it's simply that they aren't sure what they want or how to deal with what has become or is becoming of the relationship.*

SHE SAID—

"Seems like you only want this relationship when I say I no longer care to be in it. This is the nineteenth time you have apologized for the same shit, so why should I believe that this time there is any sincerity in it? I'm starting to feel like your apologies are just a way of getting past it."

--At times that is all apologies are: an escape. The word "sorry " starts being used as simply a way to get by, rather than a way of showing remorse and understanding of the wrong committed. One must know how to differentiate the two. If someone keeps apologizing for the same thing over and over again, then chances are, they are not sorry. If they were, they would have taken the necessary steps to ensure that the "mistake" is not recurring. As they say: The first time you make a mistake, it can be called just that... a "mistake." But anytime after that, it becomes a "choice."

SHE SAID-

"As I look back at the woman I was while dealing with you, I can barely believe it. Settling for less than I deserved, and putting up with more than I should've. What's even worse is that I probably would still be caught up in that if I wasn't forced back into reality by the heartbreak. So thank you... Thank you for helping me realize that I am worth so much more."

--It usually takes something drastic for people to leave a situation. That's pretty much how it goes with most people. Being "smart" usually has nothing to do with how long you remain in a relationship; so staying longer than you should is not a reflection on your intelligence, but rather a reflection of your feelings and emotions.

SHE SAID—

"I still want you. I'm just a bit more cautious with letting you know it; because I know if I put my heart in your hands and let you control it, things could be just as disastrous as last time."

—It doesn't seem to happen as often as it should, but sometimes we get the message. Sometimes we learn from recurring events that entrusting a particular person with our feelings and emotions is not the way to go, and we begin to tread a bit more cautiously with them.

SHE SAID-

"I can only ignore what is obvious for so long... before I eventually have to face it."

--*It's almost one of the scariest things people have to do; dealing with reality. Accepting the fact that it's really not you, it's them. Accepting that no matter what you do, someone will never be right for you. Accepting that it is time to move on from a situation. Accepting that your partner is not putting forth the effort needed for a healthy relationship, or that they simply just don't care as much as you have tricked your mind into believing that they do. Accepting that all those lies you have convinced yourself are truths, are indeed lies.*

SHE SAID-

"You don't seem to get it, and I'm tired of explaining. If you yourself don't respect it, how can you expect others to respect our relationship?"

--*Outsiders can only affect your relationship as much as you let them. Even with the people who blatantly try to tempt you or your partner to step outside of your relationship with them or anyone else. That door is still yours to open and walk through. The decision to do so still hinges on your will to do so; which ultimately reflects on how much respect you have for yourself, your partner, and the relationship. If you are in a relationship and still carrying yourself as if you are single, how can you expect others not to treat you accordingly?*

SHE SAID-

"I told myself I won't go tripping over this man again... but here I am again; phone in my hand wanting to call and let him have it."

--It's like no matter how we tell ourselves we are going to react the "next time," it almost always goes out the window when we are in the moment and emotions take control. Controlling your actions and reactions when experiencing those overwhelming emotions often ignited from love can seem next to impossible in most cases.

SHE SAID—

"The decision to stay or to leave has me TORN IN TWO. They tell me to move on and find somebody else, but they haven't told me how to get back a heart that still BELONGS TO YOU."

—The problem is that most people can tell you what you "should do"… or what you "need to do," but telling you how to do it is a whole different case. Imagine how different things would be if when a relationship does not work out, you could just take your heart back, pack it in your suitcase next to your toothbrush, and walk away.

SHE SAID -

"I'm not even sure if this is love anymore; or if this is just me not wanting all the time I've invested to be for nothing. I'm not sure if this is me thinking we can still work, or me just not wanting to start over, that keeps me coming back. But what I do know is that even if this is love, it definitely feels one-sided. Meaning, sooner or later, I'll also be done trying."

--*The thing most people don't consider is that we all have a limit. And at some point, we all get tired of putting so much into something that is giving us nothing in return.*

SHE SAID-

"Why should I keep trying if you're not trying at all? Why keep fighting if you're not fighting at all? I mean, you chose to be in this relationship, nobody forced you."

--People often forget that being in a relationship is a choice; because more often than they should, people get in one and behave as if they don't want to be in it, or don't care to put forth the necessary effort to have a healthy one. It's a pretty simple concept if you ask me: if you're not ready to be in a relationship, or if you'd rather enjoy the single life... then simply BE SINGLE.

SHE SAID -

"From all the times you weren't there to cheer me up, I learned to smile without you. From all the nights you weren't there to hold me, I learned to sleep without you. From all the times you never took me out, I learned how to have fun without you. So thank you; thank you for already reminding me that I can live without you."

--Always remember that you do not need anyone who does not care to put forth the effort to be a positive and significant part of your life. You were living before you met them; you will be living after they are gone.

SHE SAID-

"It's partly my fault. Because I let you get comfortable with TREATING ME WRONG; and I chose to stay even when my heart was BLEEDING AND TORN. Maybe that's why you never CARED TO CHANGE... Because I had already made it clear that I was HERE TO STAY. So maybe it's time I take us both out of our COMFORT ZONE. Maybe it's time I go find my heart ANOTHER HOME."

--Worst thing you can do is let someone get comfortable with treating you wrong, because once that comfort sets in, it becomes damn near irreversible. When people know they can treat you any kind of way without any consequence; when they know they can mistreat you and you will con- tinue to be there for them, they will often have no desire to change.

SHE SAID

"I've spoiled you with my love--giving it to you blindly and unconditionally. And what makes it unfair is that I am not getting it back from you. You might say you love me, but you take no actions toward proving that. And it sucks that I'm now realizing I am cheating myself when I am already too attached."

--People often have a misinterpretation of the phrase "Unconditional Love." Yes, true love should be unconditional, but do not be fooled to believing that is the same thing as continuing to be with someone who does not treat you the way you should be treated. "Unconditional love" is not an excuse to remain with someone who does not show the that same kind of love and respect is reciprocated toward you.

SHE SAID–

"This recent hurt and confusion I've been feeling has turned out to be an eye-opener because it has given me the chance to explore options I had NEVER THOUGHT ABOUT. See, I was so stuck on the idea of being with you that I never considered the fact that maybe I was BETTER OFF WITHOUT… And perhaps I am."

--*Sometimes a drastic heartbreak is just the reality check that we need. Sometimes that is the only way for us to take a time out and really re-evaluate a relationship and whether or not we need to continue to be in it. If not, we might continue to automatically credit the signs pointing toward an extremely unhealthy relationship to the fact that every relationship has its problems.*

SHE SAID-

"I want to blame love for doing this to me when I really should be blaming you. YOU chose to GET INVOLVED. YOU chose to LET ME FALL... with no plans on catching me."

--*Love doesn't hurt people. People hurt people.*

SHE SAID-

"Forgiving you doesn't mean that I have to pretend that you are a CHANGED PERSON. That will most likely lead me to find myself in this exact PLACE: HURTING. I know I can't help who I love, but I damn sure can help who I trust."

--Remember, just because you forgive someone does not mean you have to accept them back into your life. Sometimes you have to forgive yourself for making the mistake of trusting them with your heart the first time, and take it as a lesson learned.

SHE SAID –

"I've been there for you TIME AND TIME AGAIN.
I've forgiven, forgotten, and then TRIED AGAIN.
You have apologized, promised change, and then
LIED AGAIN. So now, the question is no longer if I
love you, the question is whether or not I love myself
enough to stop accepting the bullshit."

--Don't get so caught up in trying to prove your "unconditional love" to someone that you start blindly tolerating his or her disrespect and bullshit. Unconditional love does not mean you throw your standards out the window; it is in fact something that should be awarded to the person/people who rise up to meet those standards.

SHE SAID-

"Love took a toll on me, and I'll be the first to tell you that. Worse than losing the person I fell in love with, is trying to get myself back to who I was before I met them... before they damaged me."

--*A lot of times when relationships don't work for someone, instead of learning from it, and becoming wiser and better, they become bitter. It's almost the natural course that things tend to take. You have to make a conscious decision that you are not going to let an experience damage you; rather, you will let it mold you into a better person.*

SHE SAID-

"The only reason I'm with you right now is because you are the man I have already fallen

in love with. But that won't be a good excuse forever. For if things don't change, you will be the man I fall out of love with."

--Loving someone tends to make us give them more leeway. It's scary that even when we watch the person we are in love with do a complete turn-around and change for the worse, it doesn't stop us from still being attached to them. However, nothing lasts forever. It is possible to fall out of love with someone. Sometimes people don't realize that it has happened because they are too busy being in love with the memory of who that person once was.

SHE SAID-

"This hold you have on me has me feeling like I won't leave, ever. And all my friends tell me I should go find better; but what if I don't want to? What if all I want is for you to BE BETTER? But what if you can't be that... and I'm stuck waiting forever?"

----*It's not that easy to just walk away and forget every-thing you have hoped for with the one your heart has cho-sen. Unfortunately, even when that person is not meeting expectations, and even seemingly not attempting to, the heart still wants what it wants. So we become less con-cerned with what else is out there for us, and more con-cerned with how we can make it work with that person... or how we can "change" them.*

SHE SAID-

"I know it will hurt me so much to leave… but I won't be able to forgive myself if I stay."

--*A lot of people choose to knowingly stay in an unhealthy relationship because leaving is hard. But who said it would be easy? It won't. But imagine staying and being unhappy for a longer period of time. Someday you'll look back at that long stretch of unhappiness and hate that you didn't do what needed to be done a lot sooner.*

SHE SAID—

"It's not the break-up that gets you, it's the MOVING ON. It's hard letting go even when I know that YOU WERE WRONG for me."

--The break-up itself is usually only the beginning. The struggle begins with trying to get that person out of your system. Trying to learn how to love again. Trying to learn how to open up to someone else after being so accustomed to that one person. But the first step is accepting the situation and deciding that you do want to move on rather than sitting around and waiting for that person to walk back through the door. Once you firmly decide you actually want to let go, you'll begin to see progress.

SHE SAID-

"Friends keep telling me that I've wasted too much time on you, but I keep thinking that if I keep trying harder and harder, eventually you'll catch on and start trying. It hasn't seemed to work yet, so I wonder why I'm still hopeful…"

--*Love has a way of making people behave "insanely." For we often continue to try the same thing over and over again with the same people while hoping for a different result. Remember that sometimes some things are simply out of your control.*

SHE SAID–

"I keep trying to convince myself that I hate you just to help me with getting over you, but that hasn't seemed to work. At this point, I do not know which one is worse; what you have done to me, or the fact that I still want to be with you after it all."

--*The problem with trying to use feelings like "anger" to get over someone, is that, eventually, those emotions fade; and when they do, the love will still be there. Love is an emotion that can exceed all. Unfortunately, it's not a feeling that is easily overwhelmed.*

SHE SAID-

"It hurt like hell watching you move on before I had the chance to be over you, but I probably won't ever let you know that... because that'll make me look and be even more vulnerable."

--It's almost the worst... to feel like the person you are trying to forget about has already forgotten about you. Just always keep in mind that we are all different. We all deal with things differently, and who is to say they are over you? Who is to say they aren't just using that new person to cope? And even if they are over you, use that as encouragement to do the same and move on.

SHE SAID–

"Lord knows I'm sick of giving you chance after chance because you RUIN IT. But it's so much easier saying you will leave someone than it is actually DOING IT... so here I am again giving you your 7th last chance."

--A lot of times we get caught up in the cycle of chance after chance. And sometimes the person to whom we are giving these endless chances realizes this and uses it to their advantage. Idle threats only work for so long. Someday, you have to stand by your word, because it might be the only way they'll take you seriously.

SHE SAID-

"I hate what has BECOME OF US. And I hate the fact that this relationship going to shits only seems to be affecting ONE OF US. And even more, I hate that the one of us is me, because it leads me to believe that you don't care enough."

--*If the near end of a relationship seems to not be affecting someone, then it could mean it's what they wanted all along. Either that or they have already gotten over it. They are no longer as excited about it as you are; at least not enough to fight for it. Either way, you cannot move forward in a relationship with someone who does not care to be in it any longer.*

SHE SAID-

"This would be easier to deal with if I just simply wasn't RIGHT FOR YOU; or if I didn't care to even try or FIGHT FOR YOU. But not when I'm BUSTING MY ASS to be more than ANYONE CAN ASK.... And you just basically act like it means nothing."

--It hurts to feel like you are doing everything and more and not receiving any kind of feedback from your effort. But sometimes you have to just take it as what it is and walk away, knowing that you have done everything that you can, and they simply are not ready, or too focused on other things to realize the potential blessing they are turning away.

SHE SAID -

"If I'm going to be fighting for you, I need you to DO THE SAME. If I forgive you for a betrayal, I need you to not make me the FOOL AGAIN. These are decisions that will impact whether we make it or not; and whether I decide to keep trying."

--The battle of having a healthy relationship cannot be won when only one person is fighting it. Too often people don't realize that each party needs to contribute equally. Some also need to understand that someone forgiving you is not a license for you to go commit another wrongful act against them, but rather an opportunity to redeem yourself, and show them that the remorse you feel goes beyond just uttering the words "I'm sorry."

SHE SAID-

"Slowly but surely, I'm starting to face REALITY; and I'm starting to notice that the more chances I give you, the more you prove that you are BAD FOR ME. I'm starting to understand that you're not going to change just because you SAY YOU ARE. And no matter how much I love you, that, on its own, can only TAKE US BUT SO FAR."

-- Love is love; but, unfortunately, loving someone is not enough. Being "In-Love" takes two people. And not every-one understands that.

SHE SAID–

"I loved you as much as I've EVER LOVED. And that love turned me into the naïve woman that I NEVER WAS. And when you left, I missed you... until I tried to figure out what it was about you that I actually missed."

--The thing about it is that sometimes when we sit and think about what it is we miss about someone who was only hurting us, we often come up with either nothing, or the most insignificant things. What we miss more than them, is usually the comfort of having "someone"; but remember, letting someone go from your life who was causing more harm than good, IS NOT A LOSS, but a GAIN.

SHE SAID-

"I've tried harder; been REAL PATIENT. Maybe a bit too patient because I'm STILL WAITING.... for changes you said were coming... and for promises made too long ago."

--Some people are good at giving you just enough hope to keep you hanging on and waiting for them to step up. Unfortunately, knowing when this is the case isn't the easiest thing. Because as some actually have the intent to step up and be the partner you need and deserve, others are content with leaving you hanging and keeping you waiting as long as you are still there with them.

SHE SAID-

"There are times when I am the happiest with you; moments that I wish could last longer. Then there are moments I feel like no one is worth bringing me this type of hurt."

--It sucks when the person that gives you a taste of heaven, is the same one who puts you through hell. It's all about finding the balance and determining if the bad outweighs the good. Like they say, everyone will have their own problems. It's all about figuring out who is the person with problems that are worth putting up with because of the reward in how they make you feel, and how they treat you overall.

SHE SAID-

"It's funny how you believe in loyalty... but only when it applies to me, not you."

--Forget what has become popular in today's society; a man cheating is NOT, and should NEVER be acceptable. Neither should it be "expected" or be classified as the "norm." Loyalty is a two way street. If a man has no intention of being loyal, then why get in the relationship in the first place? Doesn't that defy the whole purpose? Our women need to accept that wrong is wrong and stand for something. Only then will they force change.

SHE SAID -

"I HATE THE FACT that when you mess up, I'm always expected to TAKE YOU BACK, knowing that if the ROLES WERE SWITCHED, you would have already packed up ALL YOUR SHIT. But every time I try to, you put up this fake fight, and I FALL FOR IT. I'm a fool for you."

--*A woman's forgiving heart can be her greatest strength and her greatest weakness; because often, people tend to take advantage of that. Know when someone is playing to the fact you are willing to forgive and is committing premeditated acts of wrongdoing against you. And even if you choose to forgive, it does not mean you have to continue to give that person the opportunity to hurt you.*

SHE SAID–

"I want someone who wants me; someone who is afraid of losing me. I want someone who gets me and still feels like they have so much to prove to me; someone who never leaves me to wonder how they feel because it's always written on their face or displayed in their actions. That's love. That's MY KIND of love."

--What we all deserve: someone who cherishes us more when they have us, not less. There is no feeling in the world better than having someone who looks at you every day like they can't live without you; like they can't imagine how they went on before you. It's what every woman wishes for. To be able to look into the eyes of her man and see a heart belonging to her.

SHE SAID–

"I had to realize that WANTING YOU and NEEDING YOU were two different things."

--Too often we get caught up thinking we NEED that thing which we only WANT. Just because your desire to have something is great, does not mean it is a necessity. And if that something or someone is not bringing positivity and happiness into your life, then chances are, you shouldn't even want it.

SHE SAID—

"I've shed just about enough TEARS FOR YOU. And I'm just not sure if I can waste any more YEARS ON YOU. It is no longer about whether you will eventually come around, it is now about whether or not I will have anything left to give when you decide to."

--*Sometimes we just have to realize that time is too much of a precious gift to waste on people who are only taking you for granted and/or bringing you unhappiness, because all that is doing is cutting into the time you have to live a happy life.*

SHE SAID-

"I'm too afraid of starting over. Too busy worrying about what's on the other side of the door I am walking out of. Too busy falling victim to my own fear of change; change that could be good for me; change that could make me smile again; change that could make me feel alive again."

--*Most people don't like change. Once comfort sets in, we often don't want to have to start trying to find it again--sometimes in fear that we might not. However, often we are so busy yielding to that fear of change that we forget that change can be for the better.*

SHE SAID-

"I'm afraid because I have learned how to deal with the hurt. I'm afraid because I've become so accustomed to the pain. Why am I afraid? Because that means I am now comfortable with getting less than I deserve... which makes me more likely to stay, even when I know nothing's going to change."

--Worse than someone getting comfortable with treating you wrong, is you getting comfortable with them doing it. Remember, YOU END UP WITH WHAT YOU PUT UP WITH.

SHE SAID-

"If half of you is the only way that I can have you, then I do not want you. I just wish that I had figured this out before I began to love you; because now, it's like I'm pushing you away with one arm, while pulling you back with the other."

--With all the complications of love, it's natural that we experience mixed emotions for someone. However, there comes a point where we have to pick a side or we will find ourselves running in the same circle for years. You can't win with love when you are only halfway in or half way out.

SHE SAID-

"Not a day goes by that I don't think to myself, 'I should LEAVE HIM TODAY.' But then I tell myself that before I go, I want to make sure that I have done everything on my end to make this work, but is that really the REASON I STAY? ...or just another excuse?"

--This is probably an excuse. Naturally, when comfortable, we look for reasons why we can't do something, before we explore the reasons why we CAN and SHOULD. If you consider leaving, more often than not, chances are, you should.

SHE SAID—

"I don't even know if this is love anymore; and I feel like you don't even know what you want anymore. Because everything you said you needed from me, I gave; and all that seemed to do was provide more opportunities for you to let me down."

--Sometimes people know a relationship has run its course and decide to continue to string the other person along just for their own benefit. A lot of times people want to explore other options but are not quite ready to break up with their partner because it pays to have someone you can always run to. Easily put, THEY ARE "TRYING TO HAVE THEIR CAKE AND EAT IT TOO."

SHE SAID-

"I just want to go back to the times when things were less complicated; the times when I had more control over my feelings because I wasn't in it so deep; to the times when I wasn't losing sleep."

--The harder you fall for someone, the harder it hurts when they don't catch you.

SHE SAID-

"Right now I'm swearing up and down that I'm done with you. But deep down I know that if you call, I'll pick up and look for any excuse to take you back."

--*The thing about love is, even when you are trying to separate yourself from someone, you can't trick your mind into believing you don't love that person anymore. You can only do your best to prevent yourself from falling back into the trap of involvement with that person.*

SHE SAID-

"They say that this type of stuff is supposed to get BETTER WITH TIME; but somehow the vision of the future I had for us is something I can't seem to GET OUT MY MIND..."

--The disappointment is more unbearable when you'd mentally planned out a future with that person. When you are forced to not only let them go, but also the thought of what could have been. Just try to remember that everything that SHOULD BE, WILL BE, and whatever is not, WASN'T MEANT TO BE.

SHE SAID-

"My friends say that I'm tripping, and I should just let you know how I feel. But I'm afraid that it will make you different... or even worse, make you distant."

--*Many of us have had that one person whom we wanted to pour out our hearts to, but we're afraid of the reaction that might follow--not sure if it would be helpful, or damaging to the existing relationship or friendship. As there is no perfect way to deal with such instances, I will say this: the only way to find out is to actually find out.*

SHE SAID

"You thought I was just nagging... but I was simply trying to get you to appreciate me while you still had me. Because I knew that once I reached my limit, there would be no turning back. You chose to ignore me, now you are the one nagging me... for another chance."

--*It is usually at that moment when they see that they are on the verge of losing you for good, that they realize how valuable you are to them.*

SHE SAID–

"I don't want to have to pretend I don't like you when I do. I don't want to have to push you away to make you want me more. I want someone who appreciates the effort and doesn't take it for granted."

--Unfortunately, this generation has become so accustomed to playing games when it comes to dating and relationships. Women don't want to seem "PRESSED" and men don't want to seem "THIRSTY." Unfortunately, this only hinders both parties from reaching their true potential as they are both forced to hold back feelings in order to play the game of "who cares the least."

SHE SAID—

"It's like I've been fighting from day one to make us work--a battle that I've seemingly been fighting on my own. But the moment I started letting go, I realized that it was in fact easier than holding on to something that just wasn't there."

--When you are holding on to something that isn't there, you end up trying so much harder than you should have to, and end up exhausting yourself. And no matter how hard you try, your efforts will be to no avail. When we decide we need to let go, we begin to see how much easier it is in these instances. You begin to feel liberated.

SHE SAID-

"...but assuming I leave, I would hate to look back and see you giving your all to someone else, and thinking that it could have been me."

--Understand that if it should have been you, it would have been you. Sometimes we need to accept the possibility that just because we are with someone at a particular time, does not mean they are the one for us. And as harsh of a reality as this might seem, we also need to be able to accept that sometimes people just do not feel the connection and attraction to us as we might feel toward them. It takes two people to be in love... remember that.

SHE SAID-

"They don't get it. All I hear is: 'if you weren't happy, why didn't you leave?' But it wasn't so much that I chose to stay because I wanted to, it was more that at the time, I wasn't ready to let go. I was still very much attached. And I knew that even if I pulled away, my heart would have been left behind... with him."

--A lot of us need to understand that when walking out of a relationship, most times we will not get our heart back in the condition it was when we entered. Sometimes we might not get our heart back at all right away. Unfortunately, falling out of love with someone is a lot harder than falling in love. However, the first step to getting our heart back and to the condition we want is to first remove ourselves from that unhealthy environment and away from that person causing it harm. Things like this happen with time. Most likely we won't get over that person the next day, or the next week... but eventually, we will. We have to be able to trust that fact and act accordingly. Stop looking for excuses why you can't, and start looking for reasons why you can.

SHE SAID -

"I can spend more time waiting for you to come around; maybe you will, or maybe you won't. I can continue to change who I am in an attempt to please you. I can dumb down my standards and settle for less than I know I deserve, but either way, I lose somehow. I guess I just have to decide which one I am more comfortable with losing: you or myself."

--Naturally, if you ask people the question of who they'd rather lose, themselves or their "partner" (who is not doing a decent job in that role), most people would choose to lose their partner as it sounds more logically or politically correct. However, very often we subconsciously make contradictory choices that lead us to losing ourselves in an attempt to preserve a relationship with someone that probably should be let go. We do this by changing so much of ourselves to please that person; or even by sacrificing our morals. We just never notice it enough at the time it is happening to give it much thought. But when you are choosing to tolerate mistreatment from someone, you are sacrificing who you are as a person. When you are making drastic changes in order to accommodate someone's preference, you are losing pieces of yourself. Granted, no one is perfect, and we all have room to change for the better; but there is a difference between someone trying to help you grow, and someone who is trying to change the core of who you are as a person.

SHE SAID-

"I'm realizing that me continuing to be this great woman to you is not the answer, because this is not at all about me. This is about whether or not you are ready to step up."

--*It's usually that simple. Some men or women are simply not ready for a relationship. It does not matter how good of a partner you are to them.*

SHE SAID-

"You were KIND when we first met. You were TRYING when we first met. You made me feel like you wouldn't be a waste of my TIME when we first met. Now as I look back and compare that to who you are now, I wonder if you changed, or if you simply just showed me your true colors."

--Some people are simply good at playing the part in the beginning stages of a relationship. They are good at getting people to fall for them, but no good at catching them when they do. Like the late great poet Tupac Amaru Shakur once said: "Watch people; because you can fake for a long time, but one day, you're going to show yourself to be a phony."

SHE SAID–

"I haven't walked away from the man you are now because I am hoping that, someday, something will click and you'll change back to the man you USED TO BE; the man you were when you felt you had something to PROVE TO ME; the man you were before you got me and said F*#K IT; the man I fell in LOVE WITH… because this isn't him."

--HOPE is such a strong force. It can keep us holding on for years; believing in something that we are yet to see. But one must be careful because it is something that can either work for us or against us. You should at least make sure that the person you are being hopeful about is giving you a reason… if not, you can get lost in BLIND HOPE. And end up losing more than just time.

SHE SAID–

"If you're not making me happy, then what am I in it for? If the bad clearly outweighs the good, then why should I stay? If you're not even going to try, then what is the point? And since I seem to know all of this, how come I still haven't walked away."

--In most cases, we stay in situations like this, even when we know all these things, because we subconsciously want that person to prove us wrong. We might even point out some of these complaints to our partner and make threats to leave in attempt to provoke change. Unfortunately, it does not always create long term results, so some of us get stuck in the same cycle of giving that person chance after chance to prove us wrong.

SHE SAID-

"I hate what has become of us; and even more, I hate that I played a PART IN IT. Seems like you just take for granted the fact that you know my HEART'S IN IT. That's why you say you'll change, but then you DON'T; because when I say I'll leave, you know I WON'T."

--Remember, most people don't believe that you will leave them until you do. Especially when dealing with someone who knows your heart; someone who knows how much you care about them. They tend to use that to their advantage because they know you will give them more leeway. Know when to draw the line. Know how to make them fear the re-percussions of their hurtful actions.

SHE SAID–

"Yesterday I was over you. Today I am back CALLING YOU 'BABE'. And I know it's only a matter of time before you hurt me again and my tears start POURING AWAY. Then I'll be back to trying to convince myself that I hate you, and that will last ALL BUT A DAY… Before I'm back here again."

-- Falling out of this cycle can only happen when you make a conscious decision that you are going to move on; one that will last beyond those overwhelming emotions you might feel after a quarrel with that person; a decision that is based off something more than just anger. It won't be easy because it requires deciding to walk away from your comfort zone and not running back to it every chance you get.

SHE SAID –

"Sometimes I sit back and think about it, and it's hard to believe I let myself LOVE YOU. Even worse, it's hard to believe I haven't DUMPED YOU. And even worse than that, it's hard to believe I still WANT YOU… after everything I've GONE THROUGH because of you."

--*In most cases, it's those trying times that create a stronger bond. But unfortunately, a strong bond being created with someone does not necessarily mean that the person will automatically change, or will no longer hurt or disappoint you. We must always keep that in mind.*

SHE SAID-

"The woman I am while dealing with you is a woman I promised myself I'd never be--a woman who stays in a situation that has proven to be no good for her; a woman I once called 'stupid'. Nothing is worse than knowing what you should do, but not being able to do it. But I guess those are the side effects of A WOMAN IN LOVE."

--*Do not beat yourself up because you fell in love with the wrong person. Or because you don't have control over your feelings; it happens. It only means that you are human. It's so much easier for us to say what we would or would not do, until we are in that situation; then everything changes. Especially when dealing with a force as strong as love which usually overwhelms all rationale. It does have a way of making you feel hopeless; knowing what you SHOULD DO but not being able to do it. But at least you have accomplished the first step, which is figuring out what your next move SHOULD BE; and that is further than some ever go. Now all you have to do is figure out a way to get it done.*

SHE SAID-

"I don't understand the shit that more than HALF
THESE MEN DO; get in a relationship and still keep
ACTING SINGLE. And it sucks that I was one to
FALL FOR YOUR TYPE; and now I'm CAUGHT
IN THE HYPE of thinking that if I do ALL THESE
THINGS RIGHT, I could change you... but these two
years of trying have shown me that that's not the
case."

*--A lot of us need to understand that people are who they
are. And sometimes that's just all there is to it. I'm not
saying that people do not change. I am saying that you can
NOT change a person. Though this sounds like a very com-
mon cliché concept, it is one that so many still fail to un-
derstand. And unfortunately, our society has made it seem
like the "norm" for men to have multiple women. So many
guys get stuck in that façade where it is acceptable to have
a "main chick," and three "side chicks"...and the women
who have respect for themselves suffer for it.*

SHE SAID-

"I hate that when I am about to walk away, you begin to say all the right things to make me stay. And I hate that you always seem so sincere at the time--to the point that I begin to forget everything I hated about this relationship. And to the point I forget about the twelve other times I was about to leave and you made those same promises of change."

--Always remember that anyone can tell you all the right things, but very few can do it. Most people know when they are about to lose a good thing, and in most cases would say anything to keep that from happening. At the time, they might even be sincere; but the problem is that when they get you back (or stop you from leaving), they grow comfortable again and settle back into their old ways. And before you know it, it's like they have completely forgotten how desperate and humble they were when you had one foot out the door.

SHE SAID-

"Sometimes I wish I was as strong as you. Or as good at pretending that I'm not hurt. Because I hate the fact that it is so easy for you to see the power that you have over me. Because all that seems to do is give you more power."

--Best thing you can do for yourself when you see that someone is taking advantage of your vulnerability is separate yourself from that person. Yes, you will think about them. Yes, you will miss them like crazy; you will probably slip up and call or text them a couple times, which is why you have to find a way to stay busy. It's not about pretending that you're not hurt. It's about finding a way to deal and cope with that pain.

SHE SAID-

"The image I have in my head of what we could be is too beautiful for me to let go; but the reality of what we are is too ugly for me to hold on to."

--*A lot of times we get so caught up in how we want things to be with someone that we become naïve to the reality of things. It's ok to be hopeful. But remember that "EXPECTATION" is the most commonly traveled road to "DISSAPOINTMENT."*

SHE SAID-

"I'm too deep in it now. To the point that even if I walk away, I am still taking a major loss. Because those years invested in you are already gone… and I can't ever get them back."

--Time lost is time lost. Rather than worrying about the time you can't get back, think about how much more time you will lose if you continue to stay in a situation or relationship that has proven to be futile.

SHE SAID-

"I wonder how long I am going to sit around and let my loyalty to you be abused."

--Always keep in mind that being loyal to someone is a good thing only when it is being reciprocated. Otherwise, you are simply being their fool.

SHE SAID-

"The truth is, I probably should have left a while ago. But I'm just not ready to go on this pointless ride again. I'm not ready to get built up again just to get let down. So although it seems like I'm letting myself drown in your bullsh*t, the thought of trying with someone else just to end up experiencing this same type of pain, or worse, has kept me here... prisoner to this misery."

--Too many times we let the fear of the unknown keep us prisoner to a messed up situation or relationship. Just remember that sometimes we need to focus less on what we are walking away to, and focus more on what we are walking away FROM.

SHE SAID–

"I wish there was a way you could know for certain that you are making the right decision when leaving a relationship. That way I would struggle less with the decision. But there isn't. And the fear of not knowing if you are giving up too soon on something that could be great is unbearable; and it creates a decision that is close to impossible to make."

—Unfortunately, there is no straight answer for this. It is truly one of the hardest things to figure out. But every situation is unique. No one knows your situation better than you do. The easiest way to go about this decision is deciding what is healthier for your heart in the long run. Whatever decision you feel like you can live with. And to help you make this decision, judge your current relationship by factoring in the PATTERN of the person you are with. Because, see, words can deceive you; even actions can mislead you; but patterns will almost never lie. If you have been in a relationship for years, you can pretty much see how it is going to be from the patterns developed by you and/or that person. That should give you a good enough idea of what you are "leaving behind," and make the decision that much easier whichever way you choose to go.

SHE SAID-

"Sometimes I wish your actions were just as beautiful as your words. Or that maybe my heart was just as logical as my mind. Because if either of these things were so, I would not be stuck in this mess."

--*Don't we all wish it was that simple? Don't we all wish that the things people said they'd do, they actually did? Don't we wish our heart responded to reasoning, and didn't love so blindly? But unfortunately, that's not the case. So next time you follow your heart, just don't forget to take your brain with you.*

BONUS

SHE SAID -

"I knew a girl. She was in love so she thought with her heart, and not with her mind. She was in love so she put him before herself. She was in love so she ignored all reasonable advice. She was in love so she tolerated a lot more from him than she usually would have with anyone else... 'She' was me..."

--*The effects of love. Don't be afraid to love, but be careful WHO you love.*

SHE SAID-

"No, don't call me 'bitter'; call me smarter. Call me the chick that learned from her mistakes. Call me the chick who has learned to read the signs and back out before I am led into a severe heartbreak."

HE SAID−

"It's crazy because she lost herself trying to find my heart...

and I lost her heart trying to find myself."

"The Down Bitch"

She has accepted the idea that "Men Ain't Shit..."

So she settles for a cheater with GOOD SEX

Minimal conversation; Maybe a FEW TEXTS

Was never real to himself, so it was impossible for him to be REAL WITH HER

But for her, his "thug image" was what made him a "REAL NIGGA"

Though he had no job, no VISION AND NO PLAN

It was ok for her, because at least they take good PICTURES FOR THE "GRAM"

She doesn't care about all the other chicks that he just FUCKS FOR FUN

She is just fighting for the right to say that she is "NUMBER ONE"

Forget going on dates; she could care less if he ever TAKES THE TIME

But when the new Jordans drop, she'll be the first to go WAIT IN LINE

And spend half of her CHECK THERE. To get him a FRESH PAIR

And maybe even some clothes that he can WEAR WITH THEM

Because see, he doesn't take care of her, she takes CARE OF HIM

And she takes pride in it; to be able to SAY THAT SHE'S "DOWN"

Because she can't stand the thought of another chick CLAIMING HER "CROWN"

But what's the point of being the "DOWN BITCH" if he doesn't hold you DOWN, CHICK?

You're just being the "dumb, naïve, going-to-always-stick-AROUND" BITCH

And, no, I'm not preaching; I'm just expressing a BIT OF CONCERN

Because after you give so much of you, what do you GET IN RETURN?

"SETTLING"

They've been TOGETHER FOR MONTHS

It started off right; spending time WHENEVER SHE WANTS

But lately she's been NOTICING A CHANGE

She can't put her finger on it, she just KNOWS HE AIN'T THE SAME

Sometimes she wakes up in the MORNING AND HE'S GONE

Plus when she texts him, he takes a bit LONGER TO RESPOND

But she's going to ignore it because she just wants the SHIT TO WORK

Couple weeks go by, and now it's only GETTING WORSE

Now he barely ANSWERS HER CALLS

So now she's stressing, tries expressing, but he doesn't UNDERSTAND HER AT ALL

He CLAIMS she's just BUGGING

Say's her home-girls are lying about all the DAMES HE'S BEEN FUCKING

Saying "Baby, they are just trying to POISON YOUR MIND"

And she wants to believe him but she can hear it in his VOICE THAT HE'S LYING

...DAMN

Now she is thinking to herself- "This whole
RELATIONSHIP IS THROWN...

Should I leave this NIGGA ALONE?

Leave one MISTER WRONG... just for another
MISTER WRONG?

Yeah, he might not TREAT ME LIKE A QUEEN, but
at least we GET ALONG

He might not KEEP IT IN HIS JEANS, but at least he
MAKES IT HOME

Plus who is to say that I'll FIND somebody BETTER?

These niggas are all alike, their MIND just be
WHEREVER

Have a good girl at home, but still be TRYING to hit
WHOEVER

Plus at 28, I'm running out of TIME, I think I BETTER

Just FIND a way to SETTLE.

"Until It's Gone"

She won't play the FOOL TODAY

Tears in her eyes, as he reaches for her, she PULLS AWAY

She says "HOW COULD YOU?!?!... I TRUSTED YOU!

You're not sorry, you're just sorry that I BUSTED YOU!

I gave you my heart; gave you my time; gave you my ALL, BUT WHY?

Because now I'm finding out everything you told me was ALL A LIE...

About how you loved me and everything else you SAID WITH EASE..."

--He tries to respond, but she cuts him off at "BABY PLEASE..."

"Don't 'BABY ME'... it won't work, this cut me WORSE THAN A KNIFE

Plus if you loved me, you never would have brought such HURT TO MY LIFE

I was nothing but good to you; NEVER LIED; DIDN'T CHEAT

Now I'm wishing that I NEVER TRIED, and we DIDN'T MEET

Because I gave you my best five years... and it's been all LOSS and NO GAIN

But I guess it's true what they say... it's the ones close to you that CAUSE the MOST PAIN

--Now as he is watching the TEARS FALL from the woman he CARES FOR, reality sets in; and now there is nothing he FEARS MORE than LOSING HER. But it's too late; she has had enough of him ABUSING HER... emotionally.

"Fear Of Letting Go"

She stays in a fucked up relationship... why?

Because she's AFRAID TO BE ALONE

Hoping that someday, he'll change.

Wondering what's TAKING HIM SO LONG

But tell me why you stay and take the pain...

When it's clear that you can MAKE IT ON YOUR OWN

I know y'all have been TOGETHER FOR SOME YEARS

And you don't want it to be TIME WASTED

But tell me, is it EVER WORTH THE TEARS...?

You shouldn't be crying EVERY NIGHT, FACE IT

If you're giving somebody your EVERYTHING, YOUR BEST

Then why in the world should you be SETTLING FOR LESS?

And you should believe in progress...

So don't even budge if they're not BETTER THAN YOUR EX

See the worst part...

Is when you know that you DESERVE MUCH MORE but you CAN'T LEAVE

Soon your HEART SHUTS OFF, it's like you CAN'T BREATHE

And you sit up trying to figure out what you put in all that HARD WORK FOR, now you CAN'T SLEEP…

Sometimes you give people TOO MANY CHANCES, just for them to FUCK IT UP AGAIN

And it always seems to start off ROMANTIC… then it leads to an UGLY FUCKING END

So when they start ACTING LIKE A STRANGER…

Suddenly their HABITS START TO CHANGE UP…

And they start taking you for GRANTED LIKE A LAME FUCK…

That's when you should start PACKING ALL THEIR THINGS UP.

"HIS NUMBER 1"

He promised her that the last time was the LAST
TIME

Same promise he has made all the other PAST TIMES

Nothing new, it's always the CHEATING SHIT WITH
HIM

She caught him with the chick he has been
CREEPING WITH AGAIN

But he never denies it; he just tries to EXPLAIN IT

Either blames it on the chick, or the girls that she
HANGS WITH

Now rather than set him straight, she will get on
TWITTER AND TALK SHIT

Claim that she is his "Number 1," and all the other
BITCHES ARE ALL TRICKS

Like – "Yeah he fucking y'all, but BITCH HE COMES
HOME TO ME!

Y'all might get him for a night but that NIGGA
BELONGS TO ME!

Y'all are just trying to break us up, but y'all chicks can
KEEP DREAMING…"

Not realizing that she is basically giving him a license
to KEEP CHEATING

But she doesn't care, as long as she has the guy she
thinks EVERY OTHER CHICK WANTS BAD

When really she just has the guy that EVERY OTHER

CHICK HAS HAD

Still she's ready to fight every chick that she thinks
has been FUCKING SON...

All for the right to call herself his NUMBER ONE...

"A FOOL'S QUEST"

So she doubts if she'll ever believe the words "I Love You" when uttered in a MAN'S VOICE AGAIN.

And she blames everything and everyone else, rather than her own consistent BAD CHOICE IN MEN.

She's been left with memories from a WRONGED PAST.

A number of summer flings that DON'T LAST.

And a few one-night stands from men that never bothered to CALL BACK.

She's hoping to find what a FEW HAVE ATTAINED; and THOUGH SHE'S PERSISTENT

She is TRULY INSANE, for she keeps PURSUING THE SAME type and HOPING FOR SOMETHING DIFFERENT.

See, the reasons for her failures with love are ALL IN ALL BASIC

She has been looking for love in ALL THE WRONG PLACES

Because society taught her that the NICE GUYS WERE "SAFE."

So fuck the NICE GUYS, the TRIFE GUYS are the RIGHT GUYS TO DATE

And she spends most of her time trying to FIND GUYS WITH CAKE

That'll buy her nice things, but never FIND TIME OR

MAKE the effort to get to know her

The REAL HER…

Now all she is looking for is somebody who FEELS
HER.

"CONVENIENT AFFECTION"

She tells you that she has had ENOUGH and she's DIPPING

So you start with all the grabbing, all the HUGGING and KISSING...

But...

Where were all those gestures to show how MUCH YOU CARED?

Where was your loyalty back when her TRUST WAS THERE?

Even more, where was your love when her LOVE WAS THERE?

Back then, before she looked at you with SUCH DESPAIR...

Now out of desperation, you FIGHT AND YOU PLEAD

But where was all that shit before she DECIDED TO LEAVE?

Where was your company on those LONELY NIGHTS?

Where were your arms when she needed someone to HOLD HER TIGHT?

Where were your kind words when she NEEDED THEM THE MOST

She barely existed to you; you had her FEELING LIKE A GHOST

I mean…

Where was your presence when all she WANTED WAS TIME?

You had a diamond but still you were too busy HUNTING FOR DIMES

And when she wanted intimacy, WHERE WAS YOUR TOUCH?

You barely told her she was beautiful, why didn't she HEAR IT ENOUGH?

Now with her foot out the door, you want to COMFORT HER NEEDS

But do you REALLY want her, or just don't WANT HER TO LEAVE?

"WHEN THE STORY'S TOLD"

When the story is told, how will you TELL IT?

Whether it's all lies, I just pray that you SELL IT

If for nothing else, then for your own PEACE OF MIND

Only regret I have is that I didn't SEE THE SIGNS

So tell them I'm the REASON WE'RE APART

Tell the world I left you damaged and BLEEDING FROM THE HEART

Fuck it, tell them I never LOVED YOU

Even though you know that my everything WAS YOU

Tell them I was a liar and a CHEATER TOO

Tell them I never tried to BELIEVE IN YOU
Go on, just tell them I WASN'T SHIT

But don't tell them a thing about the others that you were FUCKING WITH

Tell them I left you out to DRY IN THE COLD

But please, don't mention all of the LIES THAT YOU TOLD

Just tell them I wasn't THERE FOR YOU

Do your best to make them believe I didn't CARE FOR YOU

Don't tell them about all the pain that I would BEAR FOR YOU

Or even mention all the nights I shed TEARS FOR YOU

Just tell them that I'm the reason you might never LOVE AGAIN

Tell them I might have been a lover, but I never WAS A FRIEND

And whatever you do, don't tell them about me GIVING YOU MY HEART

… and then watching you RIP IT ALL APART.

"THAT SAME LOVE"

She said ENOUGH IS ENOUGH

Tossed him his keys; told him his shit was already UP IN THE TRUNK

A good girl, but at this moment, she wasn't at ALL POLITE

Said she can't wait till the morning, she wants him GONE TONIGHT

He tries to grab her, but she pulls away and says, "I don't even want to TOUCH YOU"

He replies, "Baby, don't do this, you know I LOVE YOU…"

---brief pause---

With TEARS IN HER EYES from HEARING HIS LIES SHE REPLIES- "Love?… LOVE!?!? …The same 'Love' that you give to every OTHER CHICK?

While lying and saying I'm the only one you are FUCKING WITH?

The same 'Love' that got you IGNORING MY TEXTS?

But quick to pick up when some other chick CALLS YOU FOR SEX?

The same 'Love' that keeps you out when you should be HOME WITH YOUR GIRL?

'Love should have kept you here; I've felt ALONE IN THIS WORLD!

The same 'Love' that makes you not care when my TEARS FALL??

For years now you've been the only man I CARED FOR...

See, your 'Love' must be DIFFERENT FROM MINE...

Because My Love wouldn't let me mess with three CHICKS AT A TIME
And see, my 'Love' doesn't just last for the FIRST WEEK

And my 'Love' wouldn't do anything to HURT ME

See my 'Love' is REAL... not this NEW GENERATION SHIT

That allows you to do whatever when you are in a RELATIONSHIP

And see, My 'Love' for MYSELF won't allow me to let you stay another NIGHT or DAY...

Not while your 'Love' allows you to treat me any TYPE OF WAY

"SINCE YOU'VE BEEN GONE"

I just knew life would be HARD without you

Never imagined that I'd make it this FAR without you...

But look at me...

So many nights I spent wondering what was WRONG WITH ME

Why you couldn't be mine. Why you couldn't BELONG TO ME

My friend's say there's nothing WRONG WITH ME, and THIS IS TRUE

Because all this time, it wasn't me, IT WAS YOU

Maybe you weren't ready, or maybe you JUST AIN'T CARE

Or maybe you were just using me, either way, IT JUST AIN'T FAIR

Because I gave you three years, my BEST YEARS

And all you gave me was misery and WET TEARS

At least I've slept in dry pillows since you LEFT HERE

Because the heart you swore to protect is the same one you LET TEAR

Damn...

Since you've been gone

I'm starting to notice that I SMILE MORE

And I'm doing things I never had the TIME FOR

Because see, all that time I spent STRESSING OVER YOU

Stopped me from receiving all of these BLESSINGS THAT WERE DUE

See, I MET SOMEBODY NEW; and though I'm TAKING IT SLOW

They've already proven to be more caring in every WAY ONE CAN SHOW

I guess you expect me to be mad at you, but TRUTHFULLY...

I'm just glad that after you were THROUGH WITH ME, all that shit didn't RUIN ME

But there's just one thing I've been wanting to TELL YOU IF I COULD

And that is "thank you for showing me the bad"...

...because it helped me RECOGNIZE THE GOOD!

"A WALK IN HER SHOES"

What if she was NEVER HOME??

What if she tried to sex every dude that she had EVER KNOWN??

What if every time you questioned her about her whereabouts, she came up with an excuse that was CLEVER FOR'EM...?

Damn.

Sounds a bit FAMILIAR, DON'T IT?

Well, this is about to be your REALEST MOMENT

Because after you put yourself in her PLACE and get a TASTE, then tell me how could you STILL IGNORE IT?

I mean...

What if she acted like a MAN DID?

What if she forgot what ROMANCE IS?

What if every time you asked her about a rumor that you heard, she could never give you any straight ANSWERS?

And what if every time she spoke she would NEVER SAY THE FACTS?

What if she always cheated, knowing you would always TAKE HER BACK?

———⚬⚬⚬———

What if she forgot about the SMALL THINGS??

What if she never expressed the feelings that LOVE BRINGS??

What if she was more about sex, and you were MORE ABOUT LOVE??

What if she was all about herself, and you were ALL ABOUT "US"?

What if she stayed out all night while you're steady HITTING HER PHONE??

What if you told people you are in a relationship, but it feels like you're IN IT ALONE??

See, to you,this is just a poem; but to her, this is REAL LIFE

I want to say I feel her pain, but I could barely even imagine what it FEELS LIKE.

"CONVICTION FROM A BROKEN HEART"

She's been HURT IN THE PAST, but nothing was WORSE THAN HER LAST.

I tell her it's ok to let out the pain I could TELL THAT SHE FELT.

And in her effort to convince me otherwise, as WELL AS HERSELF...

She says:

"I'm fine. Losing him was a LESSON LEARNED; better yet, A BLESSING EARNED.

I don't think about him MUCH, his memory FADES BY DAY.

No longer want his TOUCH; in fact, I hope he STAYS AWAY.

I'm so over that shit!! I PROMISE THIS TO YOU.

The thought of him makes me SICK! I VOMIT FROM THE VIEW.

Don't ever bring that SHIT UP!! That TOPIC IS FOR FOOLS!

I threw away most of his PICTURES, and CROPPED HIM FROM A FEW!

Plus his new chick ain't even cute! That BITCH IS FUCKING WACK!

He can have her BUMMY ASS, I don't even WANT HIM BACK.

Plus I heard that bitch was burning; shit; I hope she

BURNS HIM TOO!

I used to be a good girl, but this is what he TURNED ME TO.

So I don't care if I sound MEAN! He took my heart and BROKE IT!

Shattered all my DREAMS... walked away and left me HOPELESS."

----But as she starts losing to her emotions, she pauses to FIGHT THE TEARS...

But they still managed to fall; so after shedding as many as her EYES COULD SPARE,

She says:

"I'm trying SO HARD to convince myself I hate him, but that still doesn't HEAL THE PAIN.

And even with all that said, the truth STILL REMAINS that I love him.

And I FEEL IT DEEP INSIDE.

But I have to let him go, as much as it's KILLING ME TO TRY.

But I'm strong, so I'll just COPE and TAKE THE PAIN.

But when they ask why my heart's BROKE, I just HOPE he TAKES THE BLAME"

"SADLY EVER AFTER"

These are things I said I would NEVER LET YOU KNOW

But sometimes I sit and wish I had NEVER LET YOU GO

Seeing you in her arms damn near breaks my HEART IN THREE

I hardly sleep, I hardly eat. Feels like I'm missing a PART OF ME

I know y'all are together, so if I'm crossing any lines, then PARDON ME

But you have to have imagined that this would be HARD FOR ME

Or do you even have a clue? Do you even KNOW HOW BAD IT HURTS?

To watch the one you love be with another, and still be HOPING THAT IT WORKS

Because you just want them to be happy. I swear NO PAIN CAN COMPETE

Sometimes I envy her; I know it probably sounds SO LAME, BUT AT LEAST...

I have the courage to admit it. So I'm FINE WITH THAT

Just wish I could re-live all of the TIMES WE HAD

From our last day, to our FIRST NIGHT

From our best times, to our WORST FIGHTS

I mean, no RELATIONSHIP IS PERFECT

We had our break-ups and our make-ups but we MADE THE SHIT ALL WORTH IT

Maybe I got too comfortable and started TAKING YOU FOR GRANTED

But please understand that was not the WAY THAT I HAD PLANNED IT

I guess I never thought I would wake up and you'd be gone... REALLY GONE.

I guess this time I did you wrong... REALLY WRONG.

Sincerely, Her.

"BEHIND HER SMILE"

You keep telling her she's pretty, but my GUESS IS SHE KNOWS THIS.

She's heard it a billion times, so please, what ELSE DID YOU NOTICE?

Did you notice her eyes? Can you read the STORY THEY TELL?

Did you notice her struggle? Can you tell she's GOING THROUGH HELL?

Did you notice that most of the time she wears that SMILE IN VAIN?

A little more blush on today in attempt to HIDE THE PAIN...

Did you notice all the hate she never imagined she'd be FACED WITH?

Did you notice the ones that are praying she doesn't MAKE IT?

Did you notice that she's fighting? Fighting to PROVE THEM WRONG.

Abandoned by her father, another man she never KNEW FOR LONG.

Did you notice her tears? The ones she FIGHTS TO KEEP IN?

Did you notice her grind? She's got no TIME TO SEEK MEN.

Did you notice her standards? As HIGH AS HER HEELS.

Did you notice she isn't perfect? But she's PRICELESS AND REAL.

Did you notice she has been betrayed by people who POSED AS FRIENDS?

Did you notice she has trust issues now because she was so CLOSE TO THEM?

Did you notice her? I mean REALLY NOTICE HER...?

Or do you just NOTICE THE FACE...? And are you just HOPING FOR PLAY...?

"ANOTHER MAN'S TREASURE"

You NEGLECTED HER, so the next man ACCEPTED HER

When you saw the worst, the next man saw the BEST IN HER

When you caused her pain, the next man was there to COMFORT HER

All she needed was someone to express their LOVE FOR HER

You cursed at her, so the next man gave her COMPLIMENTS

You belittled her, so the next man gave her CONFIDENCE

You left her alone, so the next man was her COMPANY

You lacked support; he told her she could be anything she WANTS TO BE

You gave her sex, but the next man gave her INTIMACY

As well as passion, and a couple other THINGS SHE MAY NEED

You gave her tears, so the next man MADE HER SMILE

You gave her lows, so the next man GAVE HER HIGHS

You gave her minutes, so the next man gave her

HOURS OF HIS LOVE

You gave her birthday cards, but the next man gave her FLOWERS JUST BECAUSE

You kept her a secret, so the next man SANG IT TO THE WORLD

Either treat her like your treasure, or make PLANS TO LOSE YOUR GIRL

Because when you ignore her, the NEXT MAN'LL LISTEN

You pass up on her, and he'll make her LEFT HAND GLISTEN.

"DAMAGED"

Looking in the mirror, I swear I SEE SOMEBODY ELSE

I'm Broken; my heart's screaming "PLEASE SOMEBODY HELP!!"

How could the one who swore to protect it BE THE REASON

That my heart can't manage to HEAL? It somehow just KEEPS ON BLEEDING

I don't want to be this person; the girl that is always so HURT AND BITTER

Unleashing the pain of her past on whatever new PERSON'S WITH HER

How could you hurt me and then leave me for the NEXT DUDE TO FIX?

You never loved me, and this torn heart is the BEST PROOF OF THIS

You left me BROKEN FOR REPAIR; Screaming and HOPING YOU'D HEAR

But you turned deaf to my cry as you watched me SOAK IN MY TEARS

Now every dude after you can see the stain my running EYELINER HAS LEFT

And they label me as a "Bitter angry bitch" NINE TIMES OUTTA TEN

And maybe they're right, because fuck it, I AM ANGRY AS FUCK!

More so because I don't know if I'll ever meet another MAN I CAN TRUST

And it's not a reflection of them; more so a REFLECTION OF YOU

I'm sure there are some good ones out there; shit, I've probably REJECTED A FEW

Because sadly, now in my eyes, they are ALL THE SAME

After all, when I met you, I never imagined that you would CAUSE THIS PAIN...

But you did.

"THE MIND vs. THE HEART"

I want to stay with you; I don't want to just WALK AWAY

After everything we've been through, I don't want to throw it ALL AWAY

But I'd be dumb to stay and keep PRAYING YOU CHANGE

When your actions show you have all intentions of STAYING THE SAME

How could I love you?... WHY DO I LOVE YOU?
Why do I hate the thought of someone else TRYING TO CUFF YOU?
Why do I want to be with someone I know is WRONG FOR ME?

Why am I so stuck on claiming someone who never really BELONGED TO ME?

My MIND is telling me to move on, like "you're SMARTER THAN THIS…"

But "knowing" is one thing… actually going against your HEART IS THE TRICK

I hate when they disagree… My MIND AND MY HEART

Because though I'm better off, I still hate the TIME WE'RE APART

So I keep COMING BACK TO YOU. Why do I keep COMING BACK TO YOU?

I get hurt, then walk away, only to come RUNNING BACK TO YOU.

I keep losing years with you and it ONLY GETS WORSE

I guess it's time I decide if I'd rather be ALONE OR BE HURT

They tell you to follow your heart; but also TELL YOU TO BE SMART

But when they both disagree, how do you TELL THE TWO APART?

And even if you do, how do you know which one to choose?

Damn… somehow it seems like either way, I lose.

"FALSE HOPE"

She's been turning down every dude that
APPROACHES HER

Stays to herself; tries not to let anyone get CLOSE TO
HER

Even passed up on some good men that she refused
to MAKE A DATE WITH
When they ask her "why not," she just lies and SAYS
SHE'S TAKEN

But see, she's been single for A YEAR now because
she was HURT IN THE PAST

But she's still hoping that she can somehow make
things WORK WITH HER LAST

She thinks she's not ready for something new, Feels
HOPELESS AND STRESSED

She wants to play it out longer and see how things
GO WITH HER EX

But I wonder if she knows...

I wonder if she knows that love is not CONVENIENT

It doesn't just disappear and appear right when you
NEED IT...

Spend more time REFLECTING on your past and
you'll MISS OUT ON YOUR PRESENT

Spend more time STRESSING over your last, and
you'll MISS OUT ON YOUR BLESSING....

But I wonder if she knows... I wonder if she knows

That NINE TIMES OUTTA TEN, he isn't STRESSING OVER YOU

And NINE TIMES OUTTA TEN, he's probably SEXING SOMEONE NEW

And NINE TIMES OUTTA TEN, he probably CALLS YOU WHEN HE'S BORED

Just to sex you, then forget you, and IGNORE YOU WHEN YOU CALL

Damn... but I wonder if she knows... I wonder if she knows

That he's just stringing her along for some NOW AND THEN SEX

By giving her a bit of false hope, because that's how FOUL SOME MEN GET...

And she's falling for it... I can see her falling for it

And I want to tell her... but chances are, she'll just ignore it.

"THE LAST STRAW"

She's going to let those tears fall today, but it's going to be the LAST TIME
She usually lets him slide, even when she knows his ASS IS LYING

But she won't be naïve today, NOPE! She's going to FACE THE FACTS

See, he just USES and ABUSES knowing that she's going to TAKE HIM BACK
She stays up, so as he walks through the DOOR, SHE'S WAITING
HE jumps right into sweet talking but she just IGNORES HIS STATEMENTS
HE can save his apologies today, because they DON'T EVEN MATTER

He does the same shit, then apologizes, and she's starting to NOTICE A PATTERN

Friends have been telling her to leave, but she just TELLS THEM THAT SHE LOVES HIM
Tonight he's wearing a different fragrance, she can SMELL IT WHEN SHE HUGS HIM

And she knows it isn't hers, because SHE DON'T WEAR CHANEL

He's going to try to slick talk out of this, but ain't NO WAY IN HELL

Because she already knew, she was just waiting on him to SLIP UP

Plus he left his fly open, dumb ass forgot to ZIP UP
Desperate to plead out, he says, "I was just hanging
with my COUSINS, BABE..."

But before he could finish, she jumps in, cuts him OFF
AND SAYS-

----"Save it! I ain't trying to hear SHIT YOU SAYING!

Just take your ass back to that same bed from WHICH
YOU CAME!

You must have bumped your head thinking I'm going
to always STICK AROUND!

I knew you would cross the line some day, and you
just DID IT NOW!

SO TRUST ME, THAT'S IT!

Hope you made plans to be with her because now
you are STUCK WITH THAT BITCH!

You just lost someone who loves you over a 'FUCK'
WITH THAT BITCH!

Hope it was worth it..."

"CHANGES" (She Used To Be Happy)

There was a time when she used to be happy…

There was a time when he made her happy…

As he watches her walk out, you could almost SEE THROUGH HIS HEART

As he reflects on the man he swore to BE IN THE START

Somewhere down the road, he lost his way; either that, or he was NEVER FOUND

Because he became someone else; who would've thought he'd LET HER DOWN?

I mean, she wasn't wrong for leaving him; how could he BLAME HER?

He had done so much wrong that the shit started to CHANGE HER

See, she used to trust, until he gave her REASON TO DOUBT

Late TEXTING with girls he's SEXING; always CREEPING ABOUT

She used to smile, until he became her REASON FOR TEARS

Much as he ignored her cry, it's hard to BELIEVE THAT HE CARED

She used to stay up at night, and wonder what was TAKING HIM SO LONG

But eventually she stopped waiting up, for he stopped MAKING IT HOME

She used to tell her friends about their bond; how he would LOVE HER THROUGH HELL

But eventually that stopped too; for there was NOTHING TO TELL

She used to fight for him; until he stopped FIGHTING FOR HER

He got too comfortable and forgot what life was LIKE BEFORE HER

She used to love; some say she had just a little too much LOVE FOR HIM

Who would have thought he'd be the reason why she might never LOVE AGAIN?

Yeah, they say fairytale endings don't USUALLY HAPPEN

But she'd give the world to go back… back to when she USED TO BE HAPPY.

"PRETTY GIRL BLUES"

Maybe it's MAC, or maybe she's BORN WITH IT

Either way she's bad enough to make all the fellas
WANT TO GET IT

Can probably name a thousand dudes that WANT
HER IN THEIR WORLD

She never rolls too deep, just her, and a COUPLE OF
HER GIRLS

Everything is on point, from her HAIR TO HER
STYLE

Might catch her at a couple parties, always
WEARING A SMILE

Probably get offered a thousand drinks if she STAYS
BY THE BAR

A thousand dudes try to get her number on her WAY
TO HER CAR

High heels and make-up seem to be her CLOSEST
FRIENDS

A hundred InstaGram likes on pictures she smiles
and POSES IN

But who would believe a girl that gets so much
ATTENTION IS ALONE?

She doesn't give out her number. No, you can't TEXT
HER ON HER PHONE

Because see, the more dudes that approach her, the
more SKEPTICAL SHE GETS

Because out of every 100 dudes, 90 are just

CHECKING FOR SOME SEX

The other 10 aren't much better, Because they just
WANT HER 'CAUSE SHE'S FINE

Refusing to be anybody's "trophy," she doesn't give
NONE OF THEM THE TIME

It's the CURSE of a PRETTY GIRL

She'll only FLIRT, 'cause she's afraid to get HURT in
this SHITTY WORLD

Still she hopes to find love before she leaves this
DAMN PLACE

But it's hard to pick "the one" when everyone has
their HAND RAISED.

"MIND GAMES"

After forgetting a past and the feelings she
ABANDONED WITH IT
She finds herself re-living a battle when surprised by
a RANDOM VISIT

Now what she feels is just as confusing as IT CAN BE
Struggling to find the words to say to him, as she is
still in DISBELIEF

Now with watered eyes and a RACING HEART

And so much to let out, but not knowing WHERE TO
START

She looks at him and says-

"For a while now I had succeeded in FOOLING MY
MIND
You'd be amazed at just what you can DO WITH
SOME *TIME*

I had moved on and everything was GOING RIGHT
Even found somebody new, and he and I are SO
ALIKE

And no, he's not PERFECT

But he has a good heart, and was there when I was
HURTING

And now you show back up... why did you
FUCKING SHOW UP!!??

I guess everything you put me through just WASN'T
ENOUGH!??

Because now you are bringing back feelings that I THOUGHT WERE ALL GONE

You have me back battling something that I have FOUGHT FOR SO LONG

The URGE TO BE WITH YOU... but it HURTS TO BE WITH YOU

I want you back, and I know it will never WORK, BUT I MISS YOU

I swear you knew what you were doing when you WALKED THROUGH THE DOOR

Why do you think I keep my distance, and never CALL YOU AT ALL?
WAIT! And what about my new dude? This isn't at all FAIR TO HIM!

I fucking hate this, how the hell did I end up HERE AGAIN!!??"

"STRONGER THAN YOU THOUGHT"

Dear Past,

Yesterday I was broken, but TOMORROW, I'LL LIVE
I knew you wanted to see me bitter, so I CHOSE TO
FORGIVE

I knew you wanted me to remember, so I CHOSE TO
FORGET

For as the saying goes- life is way too SHORT FOR
REGRETS

I knew you would love seeing me miserable, so I
CHOSE TO MOVE ON

I knew you wanted to see me vulnerable, so I CHOSE
TO BE STRONG

Not going to say I wasn't hurt, because Lord KNOWS
I WAS

But hurt people hurt people, and I CHOSE TO LOVE

Did everything to bring me down, shit, I HOPE
YOU'RE PROUD

Knew you would love to see me upset, so I CHOSE
TO SMILE

Knew you wanted me to curse you; and try to bring
you PAIN, I SUPPOSE
But instead I talked to the Lord, and I PRAYED FOR
MY FOES

Though we had no contact, I could still sense that you
were FOCUSED ON ME

Praying I would somehow fail, and that's why I CHOSE TO SUCCEED

I knew you thought I wouldn't make it without your LOVE OR YOUR SUPPORT

But see as it turns out, I'm a lot STRONGER THAN YOU THOUGHT.

P.S

... I don't know of the things that I may NEVER BE without you

...But I can promise you I will be a BETTER ME without you.

"HER WORST FEAR"

Sitting in the car thinking about how things have
BEEN IN THE PAST

She finds herself hoping that this one doesn't END
LIKE THE LAST

Thinking- "Lord, please don't let him be like those
OTHER DUDES

The ones I really liked and ended up giving my
LOVING TO

I don't know if it happened too soon, but I swear it
FELT RIGHT

I tried to keep my guard up, but somehow, they FELL
TWICE

And both times, I wanted to. I mean he SEEMS LIKE
A NICE GUY

Only known him for a month, but if he LEAVES
THEN I MIGHT CRY

I feel like I've been here before; like I know how this
STORY ENDS

My mind is telling me to slow down, the same way it
TOLD ME THEN

But see, I've waited too long to FEEL THIS AGAIN

I hope this time it's different, and I can have some-
thing REAL BUILT WITH HIM

But does he even want that? Does he REALLY think
OF ME THAT WAY?

At times it seems like it; he wants to be much more than just 'LOVERS' I PRAY

Everything STARTED WELL, but sometimes his actions make it HARD TO TELL

Not sure if I should keep letting him in, or step back and GUARD MYSELF

Don't want to fall for another Mr. Wrong just POSING AS "MISTER RIGHT"

You know, the type that acts like they like you, but just HOPING TO HIT IT TWICE

Those are the worst ones, because they'll have you fall with no PLANS TO CATCH

And I just can't get myself involved with another MAN LIKE THAT

I need a sign...

"NOTHING TO MISS"

The break-up didn't sit on her MIND FOR TOO
LONG

Before she decided that it was TIME TO MOVE ON

Too young to sit around, she's moving ON TO THE
NEXT

But sooner than she thought, she gets a CALL FROM
HER EX

Same dude who was the CAUSE FOR ALL HER
STRESS

First thing he asked is "Do You Miss ME?"…

After she PAUSES FOR A SECOND, she says-

"Well, I don't miss the time that we ALMOST NEVER
SPENT

And I'm not missing out on those dates that we
ALMOST NEVER WENT

And I don't miss your kiss because you were STINGY
WITH THOSE TOO

We barely behaved like a couple; didn't do the
THINGS THAT MOST DO

I don't miss your shoulder because it was never
THERE FOR ME TO CRY ON

Love had me in the dark; just glad I finally turned the
LIGHT ON

I don't miss our love-making because it was MORE
LIKE 'FUCKING'

I tried connecting with you, but I was giving you my ALL FOR NOTHING

I don't miss your conversation because I was someone you RARELY SPOKE TO

We were together for two years, and it still feels like I BARELY KNOW YOU

I don't miss you always having to make a SCENE AND FIGHT

I don't miss all the arguing, and you always 'BEING RIGHT'

And I don't miss your touch because they only left me with a GANG OF SCARS

And the fact that you would hit a woman only shows the kind of MAN YOU ARE

I don't miss your compliments because they came FEW AND FAR BETWEEN

And I deserve to be treated like what Most DUDES WOULD CALL A QUEEN

Not to mention all the rumors I heard from a COUPLE OF CHICKS

So no, I can't really say I miss you, for there was NOTHING TO MISS."

--click--

"LOUDER THAN WORDS"

You went through so much to get her, so NOW THAT SHE'S YOURS...

How about making sure your actions speak LOUDER THAN WORDS

Rather than telling her a thousand times how much you CARE FOR HER

How about making sure that when she needs you, you're always THERE FOR HER?

Rather than telling her she's special, how about making her your ONLY ONE?

Even more than not chasing sex, don't take it from the women that THROW YOU SOME

You can't expect for her to believe EVERYTHING SHE HEARS

Rather than having to say "you're sorry," it's better you NEVER BRING HER TEARS

Rather than telling her you're honest, how about you NEVER TELL HER LIES?

You can show her better than you can tell her what you FELT INSIDE

Rather than asking her to trust you, how about you NEVER CHEAT?

Rather than trying to win her back, don't give her a reason to EVER LEAVE

She is obviously with you because of what she

already SEES IN YOU

So naturally she wants to believe you; she just needs a REASON TO

So how about making her feel that same excitement she felt when you MET HER?

How about you keep doing the things you did when you were trying to GET HER?

Don't change things from how they "used to be" or she'll start COMPARING THE TWO

And if you love her,

Those are words she shouldn't go a day without HEARING FROM YOU.

"Ms. Confident"

Some call her "Ms. Thing"; got BIG DREAMS; been
on her shit since SIXTEEN

She don't settle for dudes that won't treat her like
SHE'S QUEEN

Bad as she is, shorty don't sleep AROUND THOUGH

She'd rather they call her stuck up, than be labeled the
TOWN HOE

Her presence is felt whenever she's AROUND SO...

Many tend to misjudge her; she just ignores it and
keeps her MOUTH CLOSED

She knows they gon' talk regardless, NOTHING YOU
DO CAN STOP IT

She's just trying to live, she ain't STUNTING TO
PROVE SHE GOT IT

She's confident, not cocky; only a COUPLE OF
DUDES CAN SPOT IT

The others tend to be SCARED TO APPROACH HER;
only a few DARE TO BE BOLDER

She's hip to the games men play, so it's HARD TO
GET CLOSE

Don't let the pretty face fool you, trust me, she's
SMARTER THAN MOST

She knows the heart can be misleading, so her
GUARDS ARE NEVER DOWN

Sweet thing, even when life gets HARD, SHE NEVER

FROWNS

She got a thing for luxury brands, and DIAMOND
RINGS
So she works hard, so she can afford to buy herself
those FINER THINGS
But don't get it twisted, she's not looking for
APPLAUSE FROM YA'LL

She's confident in who she is... FLAWS AND ALL.

"PLAYING IT SAFE"

He tells her that he LOVES HER; that he's always
thinking OF HER

And that he hasn't touched another chick since the
first day he FUCKED HER

She wants to believe him; she knows that he LIKES
HER

But it's been eight months now, and he still hasn't
WIFED HER

Hasn't made it official… So she feels like he's
PLAYING GAMES

Probably got a couple back up chicks, waiting for a
RAINY DAY

SO fuck it, she's going to PLAY IT SAFE; and she's
going to KEEP SOME DUDES

Yeah, she might cut most of them off, but she's going
to KEEP A FEW

Just in case the shit doesn't work out, those dudes will
be THERE FOR HER

But if the shit DOES work out, then those dudes will
never HEAR FROM HER

Sometimes she catches him texting, and she just
PLAYS IT COOL
As long as she doesn't catch him cheating, because
she won't PLAY THE FOOL

She'll give him some time to get right; until the SHIT

GETS TIRED

She knows p*ssy runs the world, and she can have any dude that SHE DESIRES

Not to mention the men that are PRAYING FOR HIM TO SLIP

They are lined up around the block just WAITING TO TAKE HIS CHICK

Yeah, sometimes when you first get involved, you gotta LOOK OUT FOR YOURS
But how can y'all give your all, when you both have one FOOT OUT THE DOOR??

"TOO MUCH TOO SOON"

She vows not to FALL FOR IT TWICE; she just got
CAUGHT IN THE HYPE

Thinking – "Maybe if I had been just a bit more
CAUTIOUS IT MIGHT

have lasted longer. Maybe I gave way too much,
WAY TOO FAST

Maybe if I slowed things down, I could have MADE
THINGS LAST

Shouldn't have let my guard down; this isn't how it
was SUPPOSED TO BE

Feelings came too soon; didn't take you long to get
CLOSE TO ME

Knew how this shit would end; but STILL I PLAYED

The SHIT I GAINED just ain't adding up to the SHIT
I GAVE

I WISH I MADE more of an effort to SLOW THINGS
UP

Got me still in my feelings. I swear this WHOLE
THING SUCKS!!

Even more because till this day, I still don't
UNDERSTAND IT MUCH

Thought we were on the same page; I had big PLANS
FOR US

I probably would have understood if you kept it
REAL FROM THE START

How am I supposed to just rid myself of what I FEEL
IN MY HEART?

I mean I'm sure it wasn't 'Love,' but it was a VERY
STRONG 'LIKE'

So much on my mind, I barely sleep. I now have
VERY LONG NIGHTS
Sitting up wondering if ANYONE MIGHT be out
there who FEELS MY PAIN
Seems like this love thing, to some, is STILL A GAME.

"SHE HELD YOU DOWN"

Fuck "saving face," make sure you tell it the WAY IT
IS

I doubt if anyone else could have held you down the
WAY SHE DID

You forgot the PAST QUICK, faking like you been
HAD CHIPS

Forgetting she was the one there for you when you
didn't HAVE SHIT

She could've LEFT YOU for the NEXT DUDE, but she
CHOSE TO STICK AROUND

Because that's what a REAL WOMAN DOES; she
HOLDS HER N*GGA DOWN

But you BOGUS NIGGA, HOW you gon' SWITCH
UP??

She basically put her life on hold, just to help you
GET UP

Now here you go, talking about she's THIS AND
SHE'S THAT

Just because you now got a couple CHICKS ON
YOUR SACK

But when the MONEY GOES, watch how those
HONEYS GO

Guess you thought their love was real, but it WASN'T
THOUGH

They weren't FUCKING WITH YOU! They were just

'FUCKING' WITH YOU'

Think about it, when you were down, those hoes
WASN'T WITH YOU

And trust, you ever slip, and they'll be gone just as
FAST AS THEY CAME

That's when you'll remember the chick that held you
down BACK IN THE DAY

The one who was with you for you, not for your sta-
tus or the SHIT YOU MADE

But by the time you realize it, it'll be a BIT TOO
LATE.

"WISHES OF A BROKEN HEART"

As she's staring at him, she says- "I wish I didn't REGRET YOU

Wish I could forget you. Better yet, I wish I never MET YOU

Wish you weren't there that NIGHT AT THE BAR

Wish we didn't exchange numbers and I didn't start to LIKE YOU AT ALL

Wish we didn't start TALKING EVERY DAY

Wish you didn't make me blush at every WORD YOU EVER SAID

Wish I never KISSED YOU
Wish when you were away from me, I didn't MISS YOU

Wish I would have maybe kept you as JUST A FRIEND
Wish you didn't open my heart and make me TRUST AGAIN

Wish this thing called LOVE just NEVER CURSED ME

Wish I didn't care ENOUGH to LET YOU HURT ME

Wish I could've watched you walk away and STILL BE ALRIGHT

Wish when I saw you with another, it didn't KILL ME INSIDE
Wish I had YOUR HEART so that I would FEEL NOTHING

Better yet, I wish you had my heart so that you would
FEEL SOMETHING
Because it's killing me, but for you, THIS IS
SOMETHING SMALL

Wish you could feel what it's like to lose after
GIVING IT YOUR ALL

Just wish I didn't get let down, but I guess it's
NOTHING NEW

Wish I didn't still Love You… BUT I DO."

"WHEN LOVE IS NOT ENOUGH"

Can never question if I love you, because it's CLEAR
AND IT'S KNOWN
But honestly, I'm just not sure if this is WHERE I
BELONG

Trying to fight the TEARS AND BE STRONG, but I'm
sure you NOTICE STILL
That what we had is lost, we're just holding on to
HOPE, IT FEELS

like we both just cannot stand the THOUGHT OF
CHANGE
Or maybe it's just me--was never good with this
SORT OF THING

How could something that was once so RIGHT, be SO
WRONG
We both know we should let go, but still we FIGHT to
HOLD ON

Still attached; at times the thought of losing you is
MORE THAN I CAN BEAR
But it makes no sense to stay and try to FORCE
WHAT ISN'T THERE
I'd rather leave now, than stick around, and end up
HATING YOU
Surprised we lasted this long, sometimes I wonder
how we MADE IT THROUGH

At this point, there's nothing either one of us can do
to MAKE IT BETTER
I mean, we are both great people, we're just not so

GREAT TOGETHER

And as much as I wish it was, maybe LOVE ISN'T FOR US

Love is great and all, but sometimes it JUST ISN'T ENOUGH

"STUCK IN A PHASE"

She was SUDDENLY IN LOVE
Couldn't stop talking about her new dude and all the
WONDERFUL SHIT HE DOES
Most of which was new to her;

See, she was used to messing with dudes that
RARELY SHOWED THAT THEY CARE
Claiming relationships with men that'll BARELY
NOTICE SHE'S THERE
So you can imagine how it finally felt to be
HOLDING HER "MISTER RIGHT"

And not just another dude who was only HOPING
TO HIT IT TWICE

A feeling too good to be true; she KNOWS IT COULD
PASS
But at this very moment, she's just HOPING IT
LASTS
But "Good Guys" aren't for every woman, some are
still STUCK IN A PHASE
It was only a matter of time before it blew UP IN
THEIR FACE

Because though she prayed for a Good Man, she's too
ACCUSTOMED TO THE TYPE

That cheats or gives her whatever reason to be
FUSSING THROUGH THE NIGHT

A selection of men that she can't shake; EVEN WHEN
SHE TRIED
So it's back to the bad boys; it's hard LEAVING

THEM BEHIND

I mean, she's not the only girl with hopes of making a bad boy CHANGE HIS WAYS

....If only such a thing happens as often as MANY PRAY...

"BITTER vs. BETTER"

So what—you CAUGHT HIM CHEATING…?

What happens after you find out he was with her ALL THIS WEEKEND?

Maybe she pursued him, can't put it past those TRIFLING WHORES

Either way, he made a decision, so now it's TIME TO MAKE YOURS

You can shed a hundred tears, but none of that REALLY MATTERS

You can curse that man out, but it won't make it HEAL FASTER

You can sit around trying to figure out how many TIMES HE'S BEEN WITH HER

Wondering how you could have been so naïve, and keep on CRYING A RIVER

You could key his car, bust his windows; you know, FUCK HIS SHIT UP

Then go FUCK THE BITCH UP, after you tell her how MUCH SHE'S A SLUT

You could throw dirt on his name, so other chicks won't want to FUCK WITH HIM

Then let your heart turn cold, and decide that you'll never TRUST AGAIN

You can spend your days bitter and MAD AT THE WORLD

While he's enjoying life, and sharing LAUGHS WITH HIS GIRL

Baby, you can keep telling your bitter story to anyone who CARES TO LISTEN

You can spend months crying, and the coming YEARS JUST WISHING

That he was still there and avoid meeting guys any TIME YOU'RE IN PUBLIC

Or you can choose to move on, wipe your EYES, AND SAY "FUCK IT"

And start doing you, because he is most likely DOING HIM

As long as you take the lesson learned, and avoid playing the FOOL AGAIN

Work on a better you, and you'll notice it reflects on the ONES YOU ATTRACT

Then watch how, later, the same people will start WANTING YOU BACK.

"SHOULDA, COULDA, WOULDA"

They ain't want you till they SAW YOU WITH YOUR
NEW FRIEND
That's usually how it goes, they start CALLING YOU
OUT THE BLUE THEN
Telling you that they MISS YOU, and WISH TO be
TOGETHER

Forgetting they used to DISS YOU, they're just
PISSED YOU'RE doing BETTER
OLD BITTER EXES that realize that they FUCKED UP

Because they WON'T GIVE UP SEXING with others
after they had LUCKED UP

Had a good thing in front of them, but CHOSE TO
KEEP CHASING

Now conveniently, they want you when they
NOTICE YOU'RE TAKEN

Telling you all the things they shoulda, coulda,
WOULDA DONE

Saying how stupid they were for not seeing that
YOU'RE "THE ONE"

Itching to feed you dirt on whoever that they SAW
YOU WITH
Giving you their best game, and hoping that you
FALL FOR IT
But smarten up and you'll realize that their WHOLE
GAME'S WACK
They see you shining, now all of a sudden they want

that OLD THING BACK
Fuck outta here!! Tell that shit to some OTHER
SUCKER
Burns them to see you're doing better, or to watch
you LOVE ANOTHER

Secretly hating the fact that you've moved on; they'll
be GLAD IF IT ENDS
Mad because you're happy with someone else, and
nobody is HAPPY WITH THEM.

"REAL FROM THE START"

She said:

"If we're NOTHING, then we're NOTHING. If we're F**KING, then we're F**KING.

But if we are CUFFING, then make sure the others know that we're CUFFING

Don't want to be hearing rumors later and HOPING IT'S LIES
IF we happen to fall off, I want to at least KNOW THAT YOU TRIED

I'll keep it 100 so that you never have to guess what I FEEL IN MY HEART

All I ask in return is that you also keep it REAL FROM THE START
Tell me what you are willing to give, and what you are HOPING TO GET

Don't bullshit me, or play games, let me KNOW IF IT'S *SEX*

Let me know if it's *Love*. Let me KNOW IF YOU'RE STRESSED

And you're just looking for someone to help you get OVER YOUR EX

Because see, I've been hurt by people I GAVE ALL MY DEVOTION

So the last thing I need is another person to PLAY WITH MY EMOTIONS

Don't tell me what you think I want to hear just to GET WHAT YOU'RE AFTER

Just be honest with me; that is the BEST I CAN ASK

Because if we start with deceit, then chances are, it'll NEVER END

If we are building this on lies, then how can we EVER WIN?

It can be pretty simple, so no need WASTING EACH OTHER'S TIME

If we don't work, fine, but no need to PLAY WITH EACH OTHER'S MINDS.

"JUST ANOTHER NIGHT"

Pillow soaked, MAKE-UP RUNNING

Anticipating her breaking point; knowing that DAY IS COMING

The day when she won't be able to KEEP IT ALL IN
But until then, the thought of him changing is what KEEPS HER WITH HIM

See, this is just another night she'll wonder why she doesn't PICK UP AND LEAVE

Seems like she forgives, just for him to pull out another TRICK UP HIS SLEEVE

Tonight, it's just another NIGHT OF THESE THOUGHTS
Of why things don't go smoothly; feels like she's always TRYING TO FORCE them

But see, to him, it's just another night he wants to PARTY TO DEATH
He calls it "time with the fellas," but she CALLS IT "NEGLECT"

She's heard the rumors about the women he sometimes TRIES TO PURSUE

And every time she asks him about it, he FINDS AN EXCUSE

To him, he's doing nothing wrong, but to her, he's DOING NOTHING RIGHT

She had plans to be with him, so he just RUINED ANOTHER NIGHT

Simple misunderstandings can STILL KILL THE HOME

The fact that he loves her goes unnoticed because she STILL FEELS ALONE

No excuses made, but they say sometimes "A MAN is JUST A MAN"

And maybe, just maybe, he would try to UNDERSTAND IF HE CAN
But to him, it's JUST ANOTHER NIGHT that she wants to FUSS AND FIGHT

But all she really wants from him is to be around ENOUGH TO LOVE HER RIGHT.

"NOT WORTH HER TEARS"

Soon as she starts dating again, he calls. She picks up the PHONE, IT'S HER EX.

He says- "And I thought you loved me, but it sure didn't take you LONG TO FORGET"

And she replies-

"Oh, I was supposed to sit and cry over you? Are you SMOKING OR WHAT??!!

You weren't helping me advance; you were only SLOWING ME UP

You weren't making me better; in fact, you were MAKING ME WORSE

You were the reason I woke up feeling like some DAYS WERE A CURSE

You were supposed to be the person that was THERE FOR ME

But all you succeeded in doing is taking some YEARS FROM ME

If you CARED FOR ME, you wouldn't have cheated and CONCEALED IT WITH LIES

Not just because it's 'wrong', but because you knew it would KILL ME INSIDE

Why should I cry over you when the bad FAR OUTWEIGHED THE GOOD?

What I needed was a man that would cherish my HEART THE WAY HE SHOULD

And you weren't that, so FUCK IT, I don't want you back; you were NOTHING

but some dead weight; FRONTING like you were something worth CUFFIN

I didn't just need a body around; I needed a HOMIE, LOVER, FRIEND

But you know what they say, it's only so long that the PHONIES CAN PRETEND

Now I'm supposed to trip over a relationship that you didn't even CARE TO MAKE?

You weren't doing shit for me, you were only THERE TO TAKE

Now you're bitter because I found somebody else and I'm MOVING ON?

You're in my past now, and that's exactly where YOU BELONG.

-CLICK!-

"NO RIGHT DECISION"

If only someone was there in the beginning to TELL
HER WHAT IT WOULD BE
Or even midway through it to warn her she'd be
BETTER OFF IF SHE LEAVES

Maybe she would have listened, and SAVED
HERSELF SOME TIME

Can't change someone who doesn't want to; she
PLAYED HERSELF FOR TRYING
It might have been the thought that maybe SHE
COULD BE THE ONE

To make him stop chasing skirts; decide to LEAVE
THEM AND BE DONE

I mean besides the fact that she was the girl that he
SAW NIGHTLY

She basically had it all; you know, the type that they
CALL "WIFEY"

He was blessed to have met a girl like her; most dudes
NEVER HAVE THAT LUCK

But he did. No one imagined that he would EVER
PASS THAT UP

But see, it wasn't that he changed, it's more the fact
that he STAYED THE SAME
Had a faithful woman at home, but wouldn't give up
CHASING DAMES
Still she sticks around through the bullshit, though
she KNOWS IT'S NOT BEST

But at this point, she's just holding on to what little bit of HOPE SHE'S GOT LEFT

Wasting time waiting to be loved; a place every woman HATES TO BE
Because she doesn't want to stay, but feels like it's too LATE TO LEAVE

Now the thought of the time wasted only seems to KEEP TEARS COMING DOWN
I mean, how can she just pick up and go? They've been THREE YEARS RUNNING NOW

Time is already lost, so she can either keep trying to HOLD TIGHT OR DISMISS HIM
But either way, she loses… it's like there is just NO RIGHT DECISION.

"AVOIDING COMMITMENT"

I've been avoiding COMMITMENT BECAUSE...

I've witnessed 'Love' and the SHIT THAT IT DOES...

And I Just don't want to get CAUGHT IN THE MIX
That's why every time I feel myself FALLING, I
DIP...

Because it starts with me KISSING YOU, then I start
DIGGING YOU...

Then somehow shit fucks up, and I end up MISSING
YOU

So let's skip the heartbreak and TEARS FALLING
DOWN

Because you might not be tomorrow, but you're
HERE FOR ME NOW

And it probably sounds like I'm only looking out for
MYSELF IN A WAY

Because I'm saying that you can't have me but
EXPECT YOU TO STAY

But...

If you stay... BABY, IF YOU STAY

And promise not to fall in love because that's a
GAME ONLY FOOLS PLAY

Then maybe this time it can last a bit LONGER THAN
MY PAST ONES
Because see, I've been f*cked over, but I got
STRONGER FROM MY LAST ONE

But these days, it doesn't last long, so I EXPECT US TO PART
That's why you can have everything EXCEPT FOR MY HEART
Not my Heart... ANYTHING BUT MY HEART

Because these days it don't LAST LONG...
Don't want to end up singing SAD SONGS...
Said I learned my lesson from my LAST ONE....

"FIGHT FOR HER"

She's been missing you; since y'all BROKE UP, she's BEEN IN THE HOUSE

But she won't tell you that; She's HOPING you FIGURE IT OUT

She wants you to FIGHT FOR HER... Why won't you FIGHT FOR HER?

Give up that LIFE FOR HER?... the partying every NIGHT FOR HER?
Love is a battle... and she's ALREADY LOSING THE FIGHT
She thinks men aren't shit, and they are STEADILY PROVING HER RIGHT

But you were SUPPOSED TO BE DIFFERENT; she was HOPING AND WISHING

That you'd be strong enough that when girls APPROACHED, you'd DISMISS THEM

And tell them that you were taken; but instead you TRIED TO GO CHASING THEM

And anytime she asked you about it, you would just LIE TO HER FACE AGAIN

But even after all that, she still wanted to forgive; she was WILLING TO FORGET

As long as you showed some effort to change and expressed A BIT OF REGRET

All you had to do was call her, APOLOGIZE AND MEAN IT

And try to work toward changing. No more
TELLING LIES AND CHEATING
She doesn't want to be alone; she would much
RATHER BE WITH YOU

But you want everyone else; and you can't HAVE
THEM AND HER TOO

You claim you love her; well, this is your chance to
PROVE IT HERE
This was simply her way of seeing if you TRULY
CARE.

"REFUSING TO SETTLE"

They say "You seem pretty decent; educated; I'm
SURPRISED YOU'RE NOT TAKEN..."

But it's not that simple; this is more than me just
EXERCISING SOME PATIENCE.

Could go find me anybody... just SOMEBODY to be
NEXT TO

But what's the point of SOMEBODY if that
SOMEBODY isn't SPECIAL

It's more than just someone to SLEEP WITH; but rath-
er, someone worth WAKING UP TO

Someone who you know MEANS IT whenever they
SAY THEY LOVE YOU

These days, that WORD IS ABUSED; 'LOVE' is NO
LONGER 'LOVE'

I need somebody I can trust; and together build a
STRONGER US

Sex is the new love, I meet plenty trying to sell THAT
STUFF TO ME

But in the end, you find out it isn't what it's
CRACKED UP TO BE

The real thing is hard to find when sex is the ONLY
THING THEY ARE SELLING NOW

So I fake like I'm buying, just to keep from being
LONELY TILL I SETTLE DOWN

And besides, the heart is way too precious to be

PLAYED WITH

Can't just go handing it off to anybody that I may LAY WITH

Not saying I'm lying with just anybody, but some-TIMES we GOT NEEDS

Maybe someday, I'll run into the type that when you FIND, YOU DON'T LEAVE

But until then, I want who I want, not just WHOEVER COMES AROUND

I have high standards, and sorry, but I REFUSE TO DUMB IT DOWN.

"HEART FORCED COLD"

She was no dumb chick, in fact, she was SMARTER
THAN MOST

But when she loved, she had a tendency to love
HARDER THAN MOST

And love is a drug that'll have the smartest ones
PLAYING THE FOOL

If you went through what she went through, you'd
HATE THAT SHIT TOO

See, now she's screaming "FUCK LOVE!" because of
the SCARS THAT IT LEFT

After she picked up the pieces of her heart, she prom-
ised to GUARD IT TILL DEATH

She's been fucked over, shitted on, and LEFT IN THE
DIRT

Lied to, cheated on, DISRESPECTED AND HURT

Always wondered how she could take so much and
STILL LOVE THEM

But eventually she trained herself to FEEL NOTHING

She isn't the same as before; nah, shorty did a FULL
SWITCH

Now they label her "cold" because she don't fall for
the BULLSHIT

But when you've been wronged for so long, who the
FUCK CAN YOU TRUST?

I mean, at some point, you just have to say

"ENOUGH IS ENOUGH!"

Good girl gone bad, and who can BLAME THAT CHICK?

And it'll take a pretty awesome person to CHANGE THAT SHIT!

"JUST A SILLY GIRL"

You apologized the last time; it's FUNNY THOUGH 'cause I BELIEVED YOU

Now here we are again. And though I don't WANNA GO, I feel I NEED TO
I'm stuck between a rock and a HARD PLACE
Because if I stay with you, eventually my HEART BREAKS

But If I go, I'm afraid that it could HURT MORE

Don't want to lose everything that we have WORKED FOR

So tell me that you're sorry; just one more time, MAKE ME BELIEVE IT
Then tell me that you love me, and look me in the FACE WHEN YOU SPEAK IT

Because I don't want to deal with the lies; and I'm not ready to FACE THE TRUTH
So if I pretend that I believe you, then maybe we can MAKE IT THROUGH

Because I don't want to have to choose. No baby, I don't want to HAVE TO CHOOSE

Between breaking my own heart, and forgetting everything I've HAD WITH YOU

So let's pretend that I'm a silly girl... I'll be that silly girl

Believing everything you say; telling myself EVERYTHING'S OKAY

Can we pretend that I'm a silly girl??... Just a silly girl...

And I'll believe ANYTHING YOU SAY... and pray it takes the PAIN AWAY...

"A POINTLESS HEARTBREAK"

She says-

"What was the point of this? Did you get some KIND OF PRIZE?

For making me fall in love for nothing; or are you just that TYPE OF GUY?

I mean, it makes no sense to me; because you did so MUCH TO GET ME

Should have told me from the start you had no real plans of F*CKING WITH ME

But even when I turned you down at first, you PURSUED ME WITH YOUR BEST

Now it seems like all that time you were just USING ME FOR SEX

If that was the case, you should have told me; I mean, you just NEVER KNOW

If nothing else, at least it would have been easier for me to LET YOU GO

But you led me to believe that you WANTED MORE FROM THIS

Why would you make me waste my time and put my ALL IN THIS??!

Could have saved myself the heartbreak; SAVED MYSELF SOME TEARS

Saved myself from a let-down… COULD HAVE SAVED MYSELF SOME YEARS

I swear it is men like you that make it hard for women to TRUST AGAIN

Now when I meet a decent man, I'll probably be hesitant to FUCK WITH HIM

Because I can't even trust my own heart to fall in LOVE WITH A N*GGA
And it sucks more than you know because I don't WANNA BE BITTER
But when I keep running into your type, that shit just RUINS IT ALL

Makes me want to give up, say 'fuck it', and just be THROUGH WITH IT ALL

I mean, why play with someone's heart? You just DON'T DO SHIT LIKE THAT

But it's cool, because what you do to others somebody is GOING TO DO IT RIGHT BACK!"

"CAN'T BE LOVE"

She Said-

"From lack of trust, to the emotional abuse, this whole RELATIONSHIP HAS BEEN UGLY

But for some strange reason, you still INSIST THAT YOU LOVE ME

So excuse me for doubting, but how COULD IT BE TRUE?

I just don't see it; not with everything you've been PUTTING ME THROUGH

You're probably not going to like what you HEAR because HEARING THE TRUTH SUCKS

But love is supposed to be CARING, and you BARELY GAVE TWO F*CKS!

You lied on a daily basis and SLEPT WITH WHOMEVER

Not trying to put myself on a high horse, but I can DEFINITELY DO BETTER

You don't constantly bring tears to the ONE YOU LOVE...

And you don't just put any hoe that comes along in FRONT OF US....

So this ain't 'Love'... this is some HALF ASS SHIT; and I won't HAVE THAT SHIT

So you can go feed that bullshit to some other WACK ASS CHICK

One who doesn't know what love is, and CONFUSES IT WITH GOOD SEX

Not realizing that, in fact, you're just USING THEM FOR GOOD SEX

Fortunately, I'm smarter than that; it isn't REAL just because you SAY IT'S REAL

You can say it a thousand times, but if that's not the WAY IT FEELS

Then it can't be 'Love'; I'm sorry but you have to SHOW me, not TELL ME THINGS

I mean, I thought by now you would KNOW you can't SELL ME DREAMS

These other chicks are pressed to just have someone, but NOT ME

I don't want to have 'someone' if they don't appreciate the fact that they GOT ME!"

"THEY ALWAYS CHANGE"

She Said- "You started off with text messages that gave me BUTTERFLIES

For a second, I thought you were different from all those OTHER GUYS

But you changed... Should have known you'd FUCKING CHANGE
Almost convinced me you were different; but turns out, you're the FUCKING SAME
I mean, at first I was hooked on the idea of BEING IN LOVE
But sad to say, at this point, I no longer SEE IT WITH US

I mean, what happened to those sweet things you would say to MAKE ME BLUSH

It's like ever since I let you in, nothing has been the SAME WITH US

I noticed you changing a while ago; but was afraid to lose you, so I MADE NO FUSS

But I saw the romance slipping away around the same time that the DATES SLOWED UP

What happened to telling me how much you miss me on those RANDOM TEXTS?

What happened to those spontaneous dates that ended with RANDOM SEX?

I just don't get it. Why did you STOP being so FUCKING NICE?

Oh wait, maybe I get it; you GOT me and then said 'fuck it!' RIGHT?

But that's the problem; y'all don't understand that CONSISTENCY IS KEY

Doesn't matter how you got her; if you start to treat her like SHIT, THEN SHE'S GON' LEAVE

All this does is make me feel like you are through USING ME

A woman should never have to talk about how things USED TO BE..."

"US AGAINST THEM"

It's US against them; baby, it's just US AGAINST
THEM

But understand that with Love, Loyalty and TRUST,
THEY CAN'T WIN

We are all we got, so fuck the PHONY FRIENDS
THAT LEAVE

Because as far as I'm concerned, you are the ONLY
FRIEND I NEED
And just knowing that they'd be happy if they
BROKE US UP, BELIEVE...

that if I need to, I'll fight for you; I have no problem
ROLLING UP MY SLEEVES

But you have to be fighting WITH ME. I can't DO
THIS SHIT ALONE

Trying to make this house a home, and I can't BUILD
IT ON MY OWN

The way we shine, I know they've got to HATE TO
SEE US TOGETHER

But all the shit they put us through is only MAKING
US EVEN BETTER

I want to STAY WITH YOU TILL LIKE FOREVER;
they can't TEAR US APART

See, even when you are miles away, you are always
HERE IN MY HEART
I hear the rumors they spread; and I see the
SPITEFUL SHIT THAT THEY DO

Funny how it always comes from the TYPE THAT WISH THEY WERE YOU

They don't have one of their own so that's why they keep on WATCHING US

And throwing road blocks; but, baby, tell them there is no STOPPING US

What they GOT IS LUST, and what we have is THAT REAL SHIT

There is no better combination than a REAL MAN and an ILL CHICK!

"ALL BECAUSE SHE LOVED"

She was never the naïve type, but with you, she
TRIED TO PLAY THE FOOL

Your LIES BECAME THE TRUTH

Because the bigger picture was what she TRIED TO
MAKE WITH YOU

It was all because she loved…

Though you barely gave her a reason to, she still
HAD A LOT OF FAITH

Things she USUALLY won't let slide, with you she'd
GLADLY TOLERATE

And it was all because she loved…

That's the reason she GAVE YOU THOSE YEARS

STAYED THROUGH THE TEARS and PRAYED YOU
WOULD CARE

That's the reason she ignored all the RUMORS SHE
HEARD

Reluctant to accept the possibility that YOU
WEREN'T HERS

No, she wasn't stupid; she was just in LOVE WITH
YOU

She might have been blind to your ways, but only be-
cause she FUCKED WITH YOU

And though she knew that she DESERVED MUCH
MORE

She knew if she left, it was you that would HURT MUCH MORE

Might have damaged her at first, but it would have killed you in the LONG RUN

Plus she hated the thought of seeing you end up with the WRONG ONE

That's why she STUCK AROUND

Even when you FUCKED AROUND

So when you tell the story, make sure you CALL IT WHAT IT WAS

Make sure they know that it was ALL BECAUSE SHE LOVED.